SYMBOLS

PLANT CHARACTERS

Evergreen leaves

The plant's attraction is its flowers

Autumn colours

LIGHT REQUIREMENTS

The plant's attraction is its fruits

Sun

Shade

SOIL REQUIREMENTS

Partial shade

Humus, enriched soil

No special requirements

MOISTURE REQUIREMENTS

Common garden soil

Drought-resistant

High moisture requirements

Normal moisture requirements

CLIMBING PLANTS

CLIMBING PLANTS

Text by Samuel Burian

Illustrations by Vlasta Matoušová and Miroslav Pinc

CLIMBING PLANTS
Original title Popínavé rostliny

Copyright © 1997 by Brio, spol. s r. o., Praha
© I997 English Edition Rebo Productions Ltd., London

Text by Samuel Burian
Illustrated by Vlasta Matoušová and Miroslav Pinc
Translated by Olena Cikánková
Graphic layout and typesetting by Alfa
Colour separation by Repro plus, s.r.o.

ISBN 1 901094 55 3
Printed in Czech Republic.

CONTENTS

Decorate your house with a green wall

Climbing plants differ from other plants merely in that they lack a sufficiently firm stem or trunk to support them: therefore they need a support. Climbing along a support they are able to perfectly adapt themselves to it, and for this quality they are used by people for covering the walls of their houses.

Due to the fact that climbing plants perfectly mimic the shape of their support, they do not form their own contours that are so typical of other woody plants. Contours are repeated often within a species and therefore allow us to identify plants as belonging to a certain group of species resembling each other in their type of branching and growth structures. In addition to the contours, the various species also have a characteristic height which the plant reaches if given a sufficiently high support.

A plant cover on a wall spreads, and unlike plaster, its quality improves as time passes. In spring they are a lively green, in summer deep green, while in autumn many species are adorned with brightly coloured leaves. The sight of bare branches in winter can also provide interest.

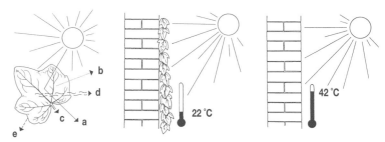

A leaf cover protects a wall from overheating not just by the shade it provides: 5-30% of solar energy is reflected from the leaves (a), 20-40% is transformed by transpiration (water evaporation - b), 5-20% is transformed by photosynthesis (c) and 10-50% the heated leaves return to the surrounding air by convection (d). This illustrates the enormous difference in the extent to which covered or bare walls are heated.

Climbing plants work as air conditioners on the walls in the wet and cold British Isles as well as in the hot and dry climate of the Mediterranean. Plant covers on the walls of many houses are over 200 years old! Their leaves protect the walls from rain, rather like roof tiles. During heavy rains, when wind drives water against the walls, the water is then led away from the walls by the leaves, and the walls always remain dry under a leaf cover. Moreover, leaf covers are not airtight and the plaster under them is able to "breathe" normally. If a plant cover is an evergreen (e.g. ivy), it works as an insulation in winter, too - rather like a brick wall about 10 cm thick.

The air around climbing plants is slightly humidified by plant transpiration, which makes breathing easier in urban areas. The leaves catch the dust raised by traffic as well as many harmful substances contained in exhaust fumes. Green walls absorb noise usually reflected by bare walls to a considerable extent.

Not even when driven by wind can rain penetrate a leaf cover to reach the wall; it is led away by the leaves without causing damage.

Some climbing plants suitable for growing on walls can bear fruit (e.g. European grape), but for this purpose you can also use covers of fruit-bearing plants trained against a wall. It is true that their cultivation is rather demanding and requires some experience but it has advantages as well. It allows you to combine beauty and utility when space is limited. Pears and peaches in particular develop into unusual beauty on warm walls, and the fruits have a rich taste.

Selecting a site

Not even the most beautiful plant can gladden our hearts if grown in an unsuitable place. The suitability of a site is determined by the four factors listed below.

Light conditions

These depend first of all on the orientation and also on the surrounding buildings and vegetation. A northern site will always be shady. However, high buildings or trees in front of a southern wall may also take away much or all of the sunshine and create shade or partial shade.

Temperature of the site

The term "temperature of the site" does not refer simply to an average temperature or the lowest temperature in winter - what counts is the way the temperature changes in the course of the year. A maritime climate is dangerous to a number of species, especially the Siberian ones. These species are used to severe cold and to a sudden arrival of spring without temperatures dropping back below freezing point. In a maritime climate they will bud prematurely, risking damage by late spring frosts. However, for the sake of simplicity, let us focus on the lowest winter temperatures, which are after all the most important. The map shows the lowest winter temperatures in the different European regions. For every species, information is given on which temperature zones

are suitable. The scale of the map does not allow great accuracy, and it should therefore only serve as an approximate guide. Micro-climatic conditions also have a great influence. The fact that temperature decreases with increasing altitude is well-known. Moreover, frost damage is also a risk in closed frost hollows.

Soil moisture

This depends to a considerable extent on the climatic zone and on soil composition. Precipitation usually increases with altitude and with decreasing temperature. Further, heavy loam soils retain more moisture than sandy soils and mixed soils. To a certain extent, soil moisture can be controlled by drainage or irrigation. The lee of a house usually provides some protection from precipitation, and such a place remains quite dry even in a humid climate.

Soil composition

Most climbers are not very particular about soil composition. There are some exceptions, however, and these plants require larger holes and enrichment of the soil before planting.

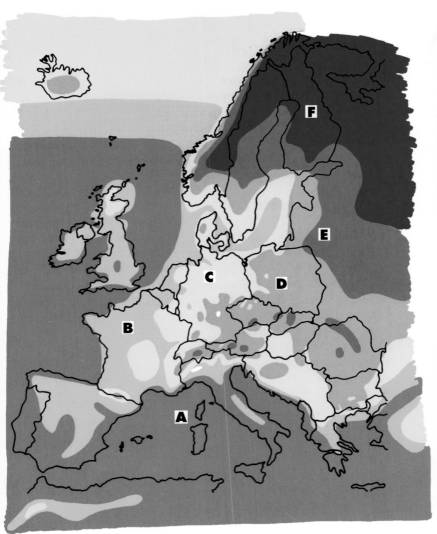

Temperature	Lowest Average Winter Temperatures in the Various Zones
A	−7 to −1 °C
B	−12 to −7 °C
C	−18 to −12 °C
D	−23 to −18 °C
E	−29 to −23 °C
F	−35 to −29 °C

Planting

Climbing plants are to grow for dozens of years at the site where they are planted, therefore the planting should be done with the greatest care. Spring planting is most suitable although seedlings sold in containers can be planted throughout the year. One side of an average family house will be sufficiently covered by one or two plants with a good growth rate.

Preparing the site

A hole for planting should always be dug measuring at least 40x40x40 cm and it should be filled with good-quality soil dressed with compost. if necessary, larger holes should be dug for more demanding species and the soil in them should be treated according to the specific requirements of that species. In the lee of a house, where the rain is kept off and the soil is usually quite dry, the holes should be better dug at a distance of 40-50 cm from the wall, and the plants should then be trained to the wall. A ground-level gutter may complicate matters to some extent. A narrow gutter may be left as it is and the plants can be trained to the wall. In the case of a wide gutter there is no other solution than to make holes in it.

Plant treatment

Plants in containers should be put into water for about half an hour

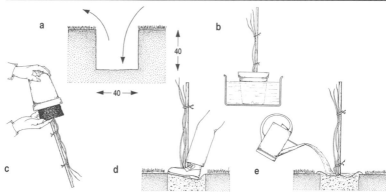

Correct planting: a - replacing the soil in a hole, b - soking a container before planting, c - taking. a plant out of its container, d - covering the roots with soil and treading it down, e - liberal watering.

Training a plant towards the wall

Planting in raised beds or the use of protective lattices protects plants from being damaged.

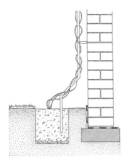

Clematis are among the best-known and best-loved climbers.

(together with the containers). They are of course planted without the containers. For the plants to survive, it is important to water immediately after planting. However, no amount of watering will suffice to wet a rootball that has dried out.

Newly planted climbers should be protected from damage. Special attention should be given to this problem in places where children play or where dogs have access to the plants.

Cultivating plants in pots

On balconies and terraces, climbers are grown in pots of at least 50x50x50 cm - the larger, the better. Double-jacket pots with water reservoirs are preferred. The soil surface in a pot should never be left bare and it should be planted with prostrate shrubs, or at least with annuals.

Runner-forming climbers

Of all woody plants, runner-forming species are least well adapted to a climbing growth. As they do not form any specialised organs modified to cling to their supports, these plants hold on in a very primitive way by merely leaning against the base with their long branches. They often use their thorns or short vertical twigs to cling. Their branches creep along the ground rather than upwards.

Supporting structures

All climbers need a support: the different groups of climbers have different demands for supports. When growing runner-forming climbers on supports you have to take into account the fact that the plants are not self-clinging and have to be tied to their supports.

Fruit-trees, such as pear-trees, can be trained and tied against "fruit walls".

Use of runner-forming climbers

It is possible to tie these plants to pergolas and trellises but they are only suitable for limited heights. What suits runner-forming climbers better is to use them without a support for covering slopes or to let them hang down from retaining walls.

It is not practical to use runner-forming climbers for high supports because tying them up becomes hard work once they reach a certain height (a ladder is indispensable). They often do not grow very high anyway. On the contrary, they are suitable for low pergolas and trellises over entrances, for rails and fences and some of them are highly suitable for balconies, from which they hang down.

Runner-forming climbers are suitable above all for covering small supports.

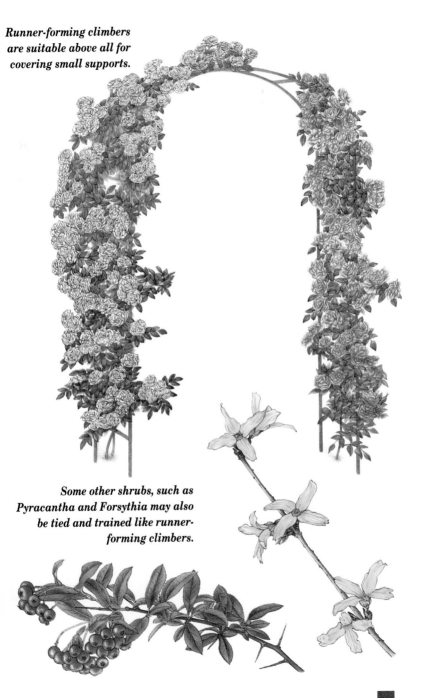

Some other shrubs, such as Pyracantha and Forsythia may also be tied and trained like runner-forming climbers.

Winter Jasmine

Jasminum nudiflorum

The white-flowering shrub with a pleasant scent which most Central Europeans take to be jasmine is in reality called Philadelphus. It is totally unrelated to true jasmine, which is a yellow-flowering shrub with impressive-looking angular branches with green bark.

The branches which form long and slim runners can be tied to or put through a support. When not given a support, the branches bend in a picturesque way and when planted at the top of a wall, they hang down. Winter jasmine is exceptional in flowering very early, usually as early as from February to March. In warmer weather and in warmer regions the first flowers may already appear in December. However, unlike Philadelphus, the flowers are unscented. They are remarkable not only for appearing in winter but also for coming into flower before leaves start to appear and branches are still bare. That is why in Latin jasmine is called *"nudiflorum"*. It is native to the north of China.

Use

Winter jasmine can be used hanging down from a balcony. It is also suitable for supports fixed on the walls of smaller buildings. It grows well in pots, too. Cut branches in a vase in a warm place come into flower within 3-5 days and provide an interesting Christmas decoration.

Site

Provided the site is warm and sunny enough, winter jasmine has no other special requirements. Suitable districts include temperature zones A to C - that is the areas also suitable for viticulture. The plant does not do well in soils that are too dry or too wet.

Contour

2 - 4 m

Cultivation

Winter jasmine does not require any special care. However, watering is desirable during lengthy dry spells. After flowering it is important to prune them to remove all weak branches and to cut back the remaining branches of young plants drastically (by as much as two thirds). This will help the formation of new, strong branches. With older shrubs, older, dry branches should be removed.

In the warmest regions of Europe, it is also possible to cultivate other kinds of jasmine - with red or white flowers.

The annual shoots are clearly angular and green.

Winter jasmine

Climbing Rose

Rosa sp.

Roses, and especially the so-called bed roses (hybrid teas, polyantha hybrids, and floribundas) are common and popular ornamental shrubs. Climbing roses are also popular for their beautiful flowers of many colours, among which perhaps only blue is unusual. Some climbing roses have been derived from large-flowered bedding roses. From this fact they also derive their name, to which the attribute "climbing" has been added (e.g. 'Gloria Dei Climbing').

Use

Climbing roses are quite suitable for portals, walls above entrances, low walls and pergolas. Flowering roses provide nectar for bees and hips provide food for birds.

Site

A site for growing climbing roses must be sunny and sheltered. However, an enclosed space without sufficient ventilation is unsuitable and may lead to fungal diseases. The soil should be well enriched with fertilisers and should contain a sufficient quantity of humus. Roses are calcicolous plants and therefore soil acidity should be adjusted to a neutral pH 6.5-7 by means of ground calcite. Temperature zones A to D are suitable. In cooler regions that are unsuitable for viticulture, climbing roses should be protected by a cover of green brushwood during winter.

Roses before pruning (a), after pruning (b)

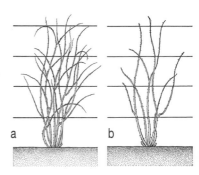

a   b

Contour of a climbing rose

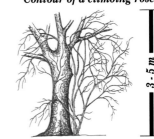

3 - 5 m

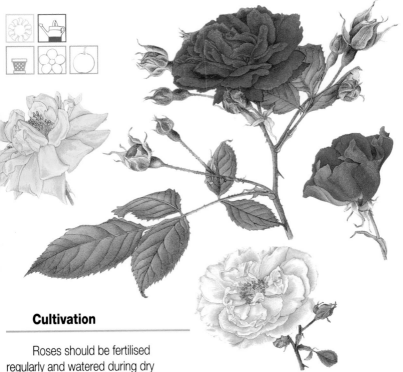

Cultivation

Roses should be fertilised regularly and watered during dry weather (do not spray water on the leaves!). In spring it is important to remove all frozen and diseased branches and also to prune the oldest branches so they will be replaced by new branches. Climbing roses are often attacked by aphids and fungal diseases (mildew). However, the plants can be protected from a spread of mildew by repeated spraying with special preventive fungicides.

Roses are propagated by budding, similarly to fruit trees and shrubs. You can also propagate them by cuttings in June and July. Usually, plants propagated from cuttings grow well, although they have a thinner root system, especially at the beginning.

Perhaps only clematis can compete with the variety and colour range of climbing roses.

Even amateur gardeners can propagate climbing roses by cuttings "under glass" in summer.

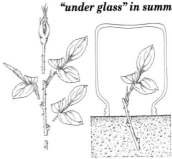

Thornless Blackberry

Rubus x *hortorum*

This is a new fruit species which has been raised over the last few decades. Its branches usually reach a length of 3 metres and they look highly decorative. The leaves survive on the plant until spring. The large, nearly black fruit also looks attractive.

Thornless blackberries are semi-shrubs. Their branches are not woody and are not persistent as in as other shrubs. Every branch lives for only two years. The first year it grows, the second year it comes into flower, bears fruit and dies. While last year's new branches are flowering and bearing fruit, the branches that will bear fruit next year are growing. The branches grow very quickly. When a plant is well rooted, they usually reach a length of 3 metres the second year.

All fruit-bearing branches should be removed immediately after picking the fruit.

Use

Thornless blackberries are especially suitable for pergolas and columns. They should preferably be planted at some distance from the walls as their fruits may produce colour stains on the wall if left to become overripe. In the garden they are usually grown for their very tasty fruit. They are good for eating fresh or they can be canned.

A shrub before pruning (a) and after it (b). In spring all weak, frozen or otherwise damaged branches should be pruned and only 3 to 5 of the strongest branches should be left. The remaining branches should be trimmed by 1/4 to 1/3.

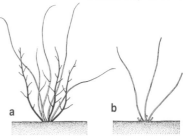

Contour

3 - 6 m

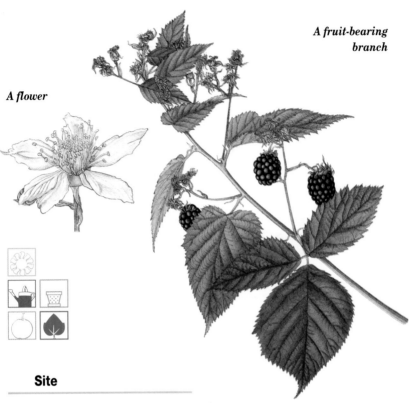

A fruit-bearing branch

A flower

Site

Thornless blackberries require a sufficiently moist site with good humus-rich soil. For the fruits to ripen well, they need to receive maximum sunshine. These blackberries can be grown up to temperature zone D - like roses. In cooler regions some of the fruits often fail to ripen.

Cultivation

Make sure the plants get enough water and enrich the soil regularly with compost. The new branches should be tied to their support right from the start to avoid them breaking when bent later. They should be pruned twice a year.

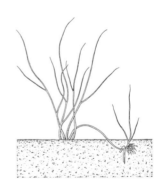

Blackberries can easily be propagated by layering. Bent branches often take root.

Henry Dewberry

Rubus henryi

This is an evergreen shrub with dense, thorny, tomentose, very long (up to 6 m) and quite thin branches. The backward pointing thorns help the plant to cling to the surrounding vegetation through which it grows wild. Its leathery leaves that are glossy deep green on top and white and downy underneath are highly decorative. They are especially glossy in winter. The racemes or fruits are of little decorative value - in Europe the fruits often do not even develop. The plant is native to central China where it grows in evergreen woods and bamboo growths.

Use

Henry dewberries are quite suitable for northern walls and retaining walls and they are also are excellent for ground cover. The shrub has rather an oriental look and therefore is suitable for "Japanese" gardens.

Site and cultivation

Henry dewberries grow reliably only in the warmest temperature zones, A and B. At a sheltered site and with a winter brushwood cover these plants can also be grown in temperature zone C (the limit of viticulture). They grow best in partial shade and also do well in shade.

Make sure the soil contains sufficient moisture and water the plants if necessary. It is better to give the plants a thorough watering occasionally than to water them too often. Thus,

Contour

3 - 6 m

Examples of suitable supports

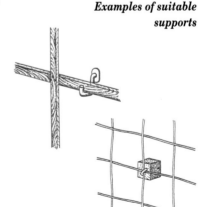

A blooming branch

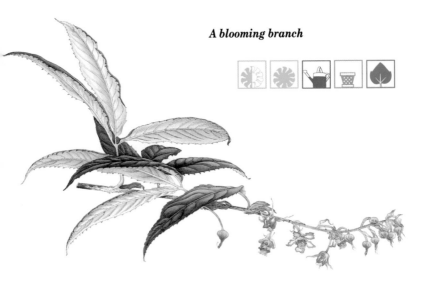

water will penetrate deeply to the roots. When the plants are given only a little water, the moisture will stay on the surface which dries out quickly and not even frequent watering will have the desired effect then. In spring, the plants should be enriched with mixed fertilisers and compost, and in summer potash and phosphorus fertilisers can be used.

Nitrogen should be avoided. When too large a quantity of fertilisers is used or when nitrogen is applied late in the season, the branches grow till late in autumn, they do not mature properly and such a plant is easily damaged by frost in winter. The branches should be regularly put through their support or tied to it.

Ways of fastening supports to the wall

Climbers with aerial roots

Climbers with aerial roots cling to the base by so-called adventitious aerial roots that are formed along the length of the branches and always on the side away from the light. The aerial roots attach themselves to small uneven spots on the base, thus fixing the plant.

Support for plants

Rooting climbers usually do not require any supports. However, the base must be sufficiently rough and it must also be firm and even (jointed masonry, rough plaster, etc.). Damaged plaster must be repaired (or removed) first. It is useful to remember that climbers protect the plaster and prolong its life but they are not able to restore its solidity and they may fall down together with damaged plaster after a while. Smooth lime plaster is quite unsuitable for this group of plants and if the climber is to cover a surface of this sort, some support should be built to support the plants. However, it is necessary to put the branches through the support or tie them to it as with runner-forming climbers because climbers with aerial roots are not able to use their aerial roots to cling to any support.

Use

Rooting climbers are best suited for covering rough, solid surfaces. The lateral branches of most of these species grow at a slant from the main branch and the plants also spread well laterally. Some species creep well along the ground and can be used as a ground cover. Smooth surfaces to which rooting climbers are unable to

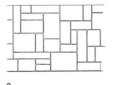

a   b   c   d

Types of base suitable for climbers with aerial roots: a - stonework masonry, b - tree bark, c - brick wall, d - Cyclopean masonry.

cling by their aerial roots are unsuitable for their cultivation. Mouldering, wet and decaying walls are unsuitable as well. On such surfaces aerial roots, which are normally harmless and only serve to attach the plant to uneven spots, may penetrate the masonry and damage it. On the other hand, firm, intact but wet masonry will not be damaged but these plants will only help to make it dry.

Climbers with aerial roots need firm and rough masonry to cling to (ivy creeping along a wall).

Hybrid Trumpet Creeper

Campsis x *tagliabuana*

Because of its attractiveness it is one of the most popular climbers, together with wisteria.

It bears clusters of very showy, long tubular flowers at the ends of strong, crooked branches from July to September, at a time when many other woody plants have stopped flowering. The different cultivars produce flowers with colours varying from orange to a rich red.

Use and site

They are especially suitable for pergolas and walls exposed to sunshine. They also look very well on columns and on bare trunks. When choosing a suitable site it is important to remember that these plants are quite robust.

These plants have no special demands as long as the site is warm and sunny enough. In sheltered places and given a winter cover they can be grown up to temperature zone C (grape-growing regions). Although hybrid trumpet creepers love sunshine, it is advisable to shade their roots, e.g. by planting perennials or low creeping shrubs around the foot of the trunk. Piling up crushed bark around their base is also advisable.

Contour

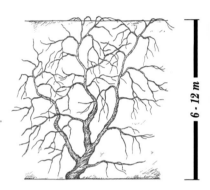

6 - 12 m

Young plants should never be covered with air-tight plastic foil during the winter (on top), but only with green brushwood, straw or reed.

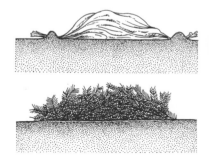

A flowering branch

Cultivation

It is important to grow a strong trunk, which is a precondition for a rich show of flowers. This will be attained by pruning. In early spring all weak branches should be removed before the plants bud. With young plants, the remaining branches should be trimmed by up to one third. With old, strong shrubs, cutting back the immature ends is enough. Seedlings raised in containers should be planted in spring to enable them to root well before winter. Old shrubs tolerate quite severe frosts and if they are partly damaged by frost they will easily grow again from old wood. It is advisable to treat the plants with mixed fertilisers in spring.

Attention: weak aerial roots are usually unable to attach the massive plant to a wall properly. Therefore it is advisable to provide a simple support (a wooden screen) for the branches to grow through. It is not necessary to tie the branches to the support.

Trumpet Creeper

Campsis radicans

This is one of the parent plants of the previous species. This creeper too attracts attention by its large clusters of long tubular flowers at the ends of strong, crooked branches from July to September. In comparison with the previous species, the flowers are a bit smaller and their colours may vary from deep red to clear yellow, depending on the cultivar.

Use and cultivation

The plant is especially suitable for pergolas and walls exposed to sunshine. It also looks well on columns and on bare trunks. When choosing a site it should be kept in mind that trumpet creeper is quite a massive plant. This species should be grown like the previous one.

Site

Trumpet creepers have the same site requirements as the previous species but they are a bit more hardy and are better able to stand a cold climate. They overwinter well, even without a winter cover, up to temperature zone C, which means that they can be grown without complications in all places where vine is cultivated.

Campsis grandiflora is the other of the two parent plants of hybrid trumpet creeper. It is native to China and Japan and it is much more delicate. It produces the biggest flowers of all

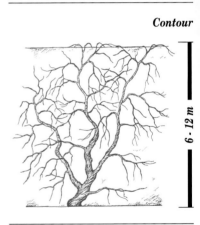

Contour

6 - 12 m

campsis species - they can be up to 8 cm wide. They are orange, and yellow inside. The plant reaches a height of only 3-6 metres and forms very few aerial roots. It is cultivated and used in the same way as the two previous species. Its site requirements are also similar to those of the two previous species, but *Campsis grandiflora* is more heat-loving and is suitable only for warmer regions (like Henry dewberry).

A flowering branch

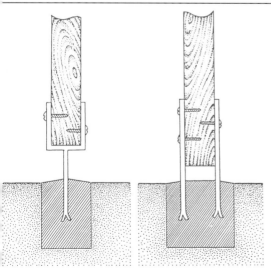

Woody parts of pergolas should always be anchored by metal elements so as to be protected from ground moisture. To avoid rot, they should always be fixed in such a way that direct contact with the soil is prevented. Vertical columns should be cut at a slant at the top to allow water to run down more easily.

Evergreen Burning Bush

Euonymus fortunei

This **evergreen climbing shrub with tiny oval leaves is native to China and in Europe it has been cultivated since 1862. The original species with green leaves can be seen only seldom in ornamental nurseries and specialised garden shops. The varieties with coloured, white, or yellow variegated leaves are much more widely grown.**

Use

It is able to cling to a rough base by its aerial roots but when it is cultivated on supports its branches should be tied to or put through the support occasionally.

Site and cultivation

Evergreen burning bush grows very well in partial shade but tolerates full shade as well. It does not tolerate excessive drought. It can be planted in all regions where vine is cultivated. In dry weather and in autumn the plants should be watered well. Evergreen burning bush can be planted in either spring or autumn.

Winter cover

In cooler regions all heat-loving climbers should be covered during the winter at least when they are young.

This should never be done by means of air-tight plastic foils - the plants should always be covered with leaves or green brushwood. A cover should protect them from extreme cold but it should not be a greenhouse where the plants

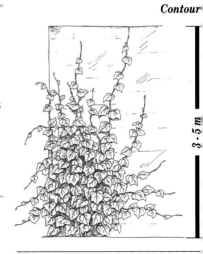

Contour

3 - 5 m

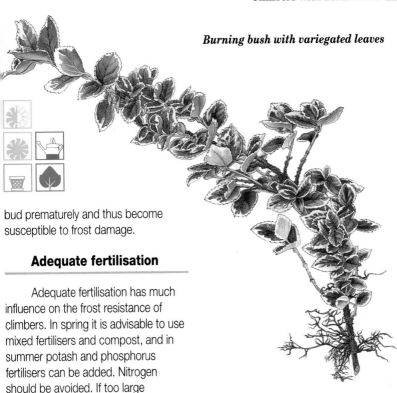

Burning bush with variegated leaves

bud prematurely and thus become susceptible to frost damage.

Adequate fertilisation

Adequate fertilisation has much influence on the frost resistance of climbers. In spring it is advisable to use mixed fertilisers and compost, and in summer potash and phosphorus fertilisers can be added. Nitrogen should be avoided. If too large a quantity of fertilisers is used or if nitrogen is applied late in the season, the branches grow till late in autumn and do not mature properly. Such a plant is easily damaged by frost in winter.

There is a great variety of burning bush cultivars for use in the garden. They differ in size, leaf colour and growth rate.

Common Ivy

Hedera helix

This is the most important evergreen climbing plant - it grows in all sorts of environments and adapts itself very easily to different sites. It reaches the largest sizes of all climbers grown in Europe - over 20 m high is not exceptional. The plant is also very long-lived - ages of 500 years are mentioned in the literature. This species is very variable and the number of garden cultivars, widely differing in look and size, is estimated to be over 250. Common ivy is native to Europe. Common ivy is a representative of the remaining Tertiary flora and the only Central European representative of the Araliaceae, the ginseng family.

Ivy cultivars show a wide variety of shapes and colours

Ivy is interesting for being heterophyllous: it has more than one type of leaf on the same plant. The leaves on the barren branches, by means of which the plant spreads, are palmate. The branches that flower and bear fruit lose their climbing nature - they are shorter and upright and their leaves are entire and lanceolate.

Use

The plant is quite suitable for rough walls, pergolas, fences and old trees. It is able to cling to rough bases by means of its aerial roots but when it is to cover pergolas and fences its branches should be tied to or put through the supports occasionally. It is the most widely used soil-covering plant for shady situations where lawns cannot be cultivated. It is also suitable for being raised in pots.

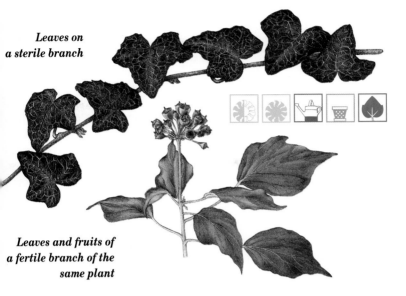

Leaves on a sterile branch

Leaves and fruits of a fertile branch of the same plant

Attention - ivy is poisonous. Its black fruits especially are extremely poisonous.

Site and cultivation

Common ivy is quite undemanding. It can be raised practically everywhere except very dry places fully exposed to sunshine. It is very hardy and at the places protected from winter sunshine it also grows in temperature zone E. However, you should take into account the great differences between the various cultivars - cultivars native to warmer regions may not do well elsewhere.

Contour

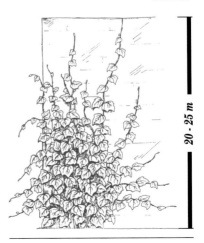

In winter, an evergreen ivy cover protects any wall from cold wind.

20 - 25 m

Persian Ivy

Hedera colchica

This plant is very similar to the previous species but it grows faster and its leaves are larger - they may reach a size of 20 cm. The plant is native to south-eastern Europe and Asia Minor.

Use

It grows very well along rough walls, pergolas, fences and old trees. It is able to cling to rough bases by means of its aerial roots but by pergolas and fences its branches should be tied to or put through the supports occasionally. In shady positions it is excellent for ground cover. It also grows very well in pots. This species, too, provides food for bees and birds.

Site

In its site requirements it is similar to common ivy. Although Persian ivy grows in any kind of common garden soil, humus-rich soils are the most suitable for its cultivation. The plant does not tolerate excessive drought. It is heat-loving and in temperature zone D it only grows at sites protected from freezing winds and winter sunshine.

Cultivation

In dry weather and in autumn the plants should be watered well. Their frost resistance depends on the right fertilisation - described in the chapter on evergreen burning bush.

There are wider differences among the cultivars of both common ivy and Persian ivy than there is between the species, which are quite similar. Some forms are much more delicate than the original species and can only be grown in the warmest regions or even only as indoor plants. Therefore when buying them you should always ask whether the chosen cultivar is suitable for your purposes.

Contour

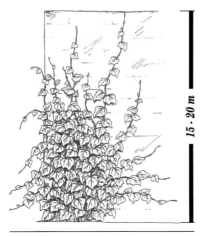

15 - 20 m

A heterophyllous form of Persian ivy

Impressive evergreen leaves are typical of the original form of Persian ivy.

Climbing Hydrangea

Hydrangea petiolaris

This is the only Hydrangea species cultivated as a climbing plant. The overwhelming majority of other Hydrangea species are trees or shrubs and some are also known as pot plants.

Climbing hydrangea is a most attractive and undemanding rooting climber. It flowers at the beginning of summer. The flattish heads of cream-coloured flowers have a number of sterile flowers with enlarged perianth round their peripheries. In autumn the leaves turn golden and yellow. Climbing hydrangea is native to Asia where it is at home in Japan, Korea, Taiwan, and on the isle of Sakhalin.

Use

The plant is quite suitable for walls, pergolas and old trees but it also makes a good ground cover. It clings to rough masonry easily and quite firmly by means of its fine, but dense aerial roots and is able to form and maintain a flat cover by itself. As a flowering shrub it provides nectar for bees.

Site

Climbing hydrangea likes partial shade but it tolerates deeper shade as well. It requires rather acid and well-drained soils with a sufficient humus content. Therefore you should dig larger holes when planting this species and

Part of a branch with aerial roots

Contour

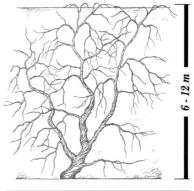

6 - 12 m

completely replace the soil in them or at least enrich it with compost and peat that tests to acid. High air humidity is very beneficial to hydrangeas. They are quite hardy and may also be planted in temperature zone D.

Cultivation

The plant does not require any special care apart from watering. It does not tolerate heavy, wet soil, but that does not mean that it does not need plenty of moisture. Therefore you should make sure the soil contains sufficient moisture, and water the plant if necessary. Hydrangea can be planted either in spring or in autumn. If required it can easily be trained by pruning.

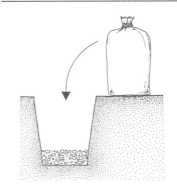

On heavy soils you should dig large holes (120 cm) for planting climbing hydrangea, spread gravel at the bottom to make drainage and enrich the soil with peat.

Inflorescence

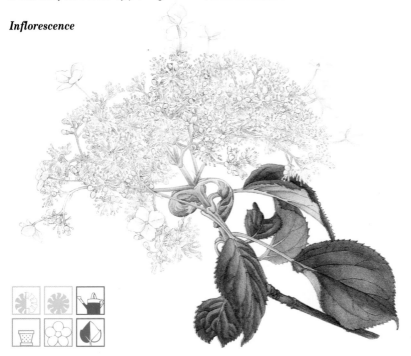

Japanese Hydrangea Vine

Schizophragma hydrangeoides

This is a most attractive and modest rooting climber which is very similar to climbing hydrangea. At the beginning of summer it bears flattish flower heads that are remarkable in particular for their marginal sterile flowers. The flowers have only one developed perianth segment, but it is large and purely white. Japanese hydrangea vine is native to Asia where it grows in the mountain forests of central Japan.

Use

The plant is quite suitable for walls, pergolas and old trees but it may also be used as a ground cover. Similarly to climbing hydrangea it clings to rough masonry easily and very firmly by means of its fine, but dense aerial roots, and is able to form and maintain a flat cover by itself.

Site

The plant likes partial shade and unlike climbing hydrangea it also tolerates sunshine. It requires rather acid and well-drained soils with a sufficient humus content. Holes for planting should be prepared on heavy soils as for climbing hydrangea. Japanese hydrangea vine is more heat-loving than climbing hydrangea and can be grown only in grape-growing regions. High air humidity is also beneficial to Japanese hydrangea vine.

Cultivation

The plant does not require any additional special care. Just make sure the soil contains sufficient moisture

Contour

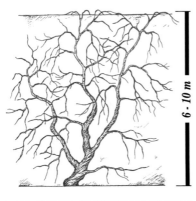

6 - 10 m

Inflorescences of Japanese hydrangea vine are more impressive than those the of related climbing hydrangea.

and give more water in dry weather. Thus, water penetrates deep to the roots and watering need not be repeated too often. If the plants are watered with a small quantity of water, only the soil surface remains wet, the roots dry very quickly and not even frequent watering will have the desired effect.

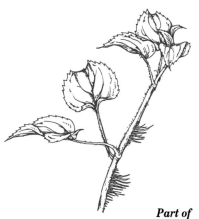

Part of a branch with adventitious roots

Twining climbers

Twining climbers do not form any specialised clinging organs, but their branches are adapted for twining (twisting) around a support. These plants are not able to cling to a surface without help and you should therefore provide supports on the walls for them.

Support should allow the growing branches to twist freely around them. Therefore there should be sufficient space between the wall and the support. A distance of 15-20 cm, or larger - about 30 cm, may be regarded as a minimum.

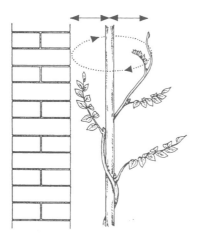

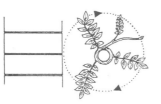

Supports

The supports for this group of woody plants should consist mostly of elements oriented vertically or at a slant. The branches do not tend to creep along the horizontal parts of the support. Usually, one vertical bar or a rope stretched tight in a vertical position will suffice. The supports can be made of any material - wooden battens, metal bars, steel wire or nylon strings. If the support is too smooth, the plants slide down. Therefore you should tie a couple of knots in every string. The metal supports manufactured by some firms are ideal. Vertical elements have slide-proof stops and they have been coated with an anti-corrosion layer. As far as wooden supports are concerned it is important not to forget to impregnate them, as the supports will have to last for a number of years and it is difficult or even impossible to renew the paint later on.

Use of twining climbers

Twining species are not suitable for covering continuous surfaces because they are usually unable to

Wisteria is among the most beautiful twining climbers.

cover horizontal elements. The branches which do not find a suitable support begin overhanging by their weight and the plant stops growing, which is typical of most twining species. This is not necessarily a fault because a number of plants flower just on these lateral horizontal or overhanging branches. Gutter pipes and young trees are quite unsuitable as supports because they may become distorted under the pressure of a thickening twining climber.

This diagram shows you how to fix a wooden batten (left) and how to fix and tighten a steel wire (right).

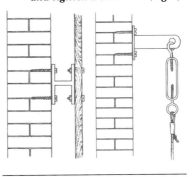

Bower Actinidia

Actinidia arguta

Bower actinidia comes into flower in June. The white and slightly scented flowers are dioecious. Therefore actinidia bears fruit only when male and female specimens grow next to each other. The plant bears smooth berries, about 2.5 cm long, which resemble gooseberries. The berries are edible and their taste is very similar to that of kiwi. Therefore bower actinidia is sometimes also called "small kiwi". The plant grows very fast.

Use

Bower actinidia is especially suitable for pergolas and walls. It also looks beautiful on columns and on the trunks of old trees. It provides food for bees an birds.

Site

The plant has no special requirements, it only needs partial shade and enough moisture. It prefers humus and rather acid soils but it also grows in any kind of common garden soil. It is quite hardy and can also be grown in temperature zone D. In winter it tolerates temperatures below -20 °C without suffering damage. Problems arise in maritime climates in spring when the plant wakes up prematurely and starts budding too early. Then late spring frosts usually burn the newly sprouted branches. Such plants usually grow again but they do not flower any more.

Contour

8 - 12 m

Cultivation

The plant does not require any special care. When there is a need to train the plant by pruning this should never be done in spring but preferably in summer. Winter pruning is also possible but it must be done in time. In spring the plants lose a lot of sap when they are pruned, which exhausts them

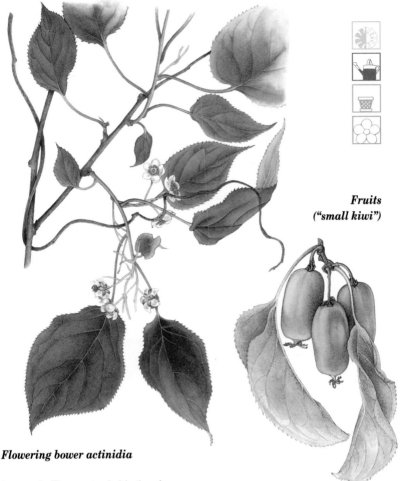

*Fruits
("small kiwi")*

Flowering bower actinidia

too much. The most suitable time for planting is spring.

The cultivars that are on the market today bear larger fruits and some cultivars have been cultivated with both male and female flowers on one plant so that it is not necessary to grow male and female plants separately. If actinidia is to be grown for its fruit too, it is advisable to buy only plants marked with the cultivar name and to avoid seedlings of uncertain sex.

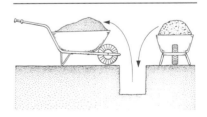

When planting actinidia replace part of soil with peat and compost.

41

Chinese Gooseberry - Kiwi

Actinidia chinensis

This is a very vigorously growing twining climber which has large hairy leaves and beautiful orange and white flowers that reach a diameter of up to 4 cm. Nowadays, its fruit is known throughout the world as kiwi.

In warm districts you may be able to produce this well-known fruit when you grow plants of both sexes (or modern monoecious cultivars).

The history of kiwi cultivation did not begin in its native China, but in New Zealand, where the plant was introduced as Chinese gooseberry around the year 1900.

Site and use

Kiwi requires a site with good, humus-rich, sufficiently moist soil, and sunshine or partial shade. Before planting actinidia the soil should be enriched with compost of a good quality and the soil acidity should be adjusted to pH 4.5-5.5 by means of peat. Kiwi is a heat-loving plant and it can be grown only in sheltered places in vine-growing regions.

Kiwi is particularly suitable for pergolas, retaining walls and walls. When in flower, it provides nectar for bees.

Cultivation

The soil should contain sufficient moisture and it is advisable to enrich

Flowering kiwi

the soil with organic fertilisers occasionally. Part of the branches should be trained along a support horizontally, and the short side branches should be treated carefully because they are vital to flowering and fruiting. This fact should also be kept in mind while pruning. Pruning should never be carried out in spring but preferably in summer. Winter pruning is also possible if it is done in time. In spring, the plants lose a lot of sap when they are pruned, which exhausts them too much. Chinese gooseberry should be planted in spring to enable the young plants to root well and become stronger before winter. It is also advisable to cover the young plants with leaves and green brushwood for the winter.

Contour

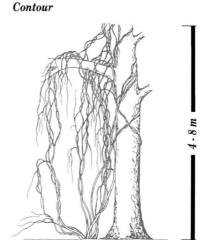

4 - 8 m

Kolomikta

Actinidia kolomikta

Kolomikta bears tiny edible fruits that look and taste very similar to those of bower actinidia, but the plant does not grow so vigorously. Its white, slightly scented flowers develop in June and are dioecious as in all actinidias. Therefore kolomikta bears fruit only when male and female specimens are planted together. The leaves of the male plants often start out half white and become tinged with pink later. Kolomikta is native to Asia.

Use and site

It is particularly suitable for pergolas, retaining walls and walls. It also looks well on columns and fences. The plant provides nectar for bees and fruits for birds. Kolomikta likes the same sites as bower actinidia.

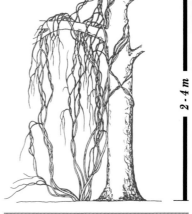

Contour

2 - 4 m

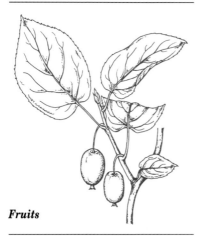

Fruits

Cultivation

The soil should contain sufficient moisture. If it is necessary to prune the plant, this should never be done in spring (as with the previous species). The most suitable time for planting is spring.

A branch of a male plant

A flowering female plant

A vitamin bomb

It is no exaggeration to use these words for the fruits of all actinidias. That is also part of the reason why kiwis are so popular, in addition to their good taste. However, Chinese gooseberry or kiwi is very delicate and in Europe it can be grown only in the warmest regions. Small-fruited species - bower actinidia and kolomikta - are much more hardy and they contain even more vitamin C than large kiwi fruits. These two small-fruited species attracted the attention of I.V. Mitchurin, who collected their seeds in Siberia and produced several fruit cultivars by selective breeding. The new, fully hardy cultivars bear walnut-sized fruits.

Fiveleaf Akebia

Akebia quinata

This is a twining climber with a fine structure. Sometimes its flowers are obscured by the leaves and therefore may not easily be spotted, but their very pleasant scent betrays them. The light purple fruits are also interesting. The fine foliage remains on the plant until late in winter and usually falls only after the arrival of severe frost. In warm regions and during mild winters it sometimes stays on the plant.

Use

The plant is quite suitable for pergolas, retaining walls and walls. It twines well over fences, screening them from view. It is also useful to cover columns, poles and old trees. It is a melliferous plant.

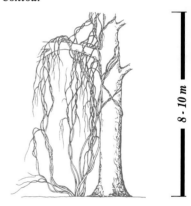

Contour

8 - 10 m

Leaves of fiveleaf akebia

Leaves of Akebia trifoliata

Site

It likes places in the sunshine or partial shade. It does well in any kind of common soil. In good soil which contains sufficient moisture it grows very vigorously and its new branches may reach a length of several metres within a year. Akebia can be grown in sheltered places up to temperature zone D.

Flowering fiveleaf akebia

Cultivation

When it spreads too much, it may be pruned as required without any problems. It tolerates pruning very well. Older specimens are fully hardy in temperature zone D and warmer zones, but the young plants should be covered with leaves and green brushwood for the winter. The seedlings are best planted in spring.

Akebia trifoliata differs from the previous species by its trifoliolate leaves, pale purple fruits and dark unscented flowers. It reaches a lower height (about 6 m only). Sometimes *Akebia* x *pentaphylla*, the cross of the two previous species, is found. It is cultivated in the same way as fiveleaf akebia.

Fruits of fiveleaf akebia are up to 10 cm long.

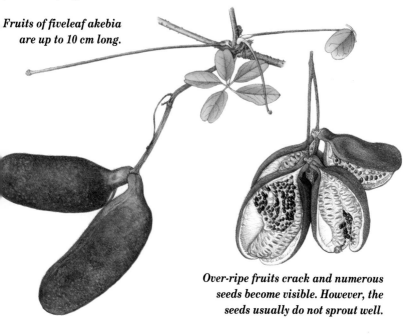

Over-ripe fruits crack and numerous seeds become visible. However, the seeds usually do not sprout well.

Dutchman's Pipe

Aristolochia macrophylla

The plant is native to the eastern part of the US. It is remarkable for its large, decorative heart-shaped leaves. The young plants do not grow very vigorously for the first 2-3 years after planting, but later on, branches may exceed a length of two metres. Dutchman's pipe is said to reach a height of 20 m. The Dutchman's pipe's flowers are tiny and are only remarkable for their pipe-like shape. The wood has a pleasant scent when bruised.

About 300-350 species of Aristolochia are known, of which only a minority are climbing plants.

Aristolochia clematitis is found growing wild in the warmer regions of Europe. It is not a climber, and is only about half a meter high. It is poisonous but its active substances have wound-healing properties and therefore have pharmaceutical applications.

Use and site

Dutchman's pipe is particularly suitable for pergolas and walls in shaded positions. It also looks well on columns and tree trunks. It is good at screening fences from view.

Dutchman's pipe requires sites that are sufficiently moist because its large leaves evaporate a lot of water. The plant prefers partial shade but it

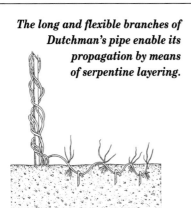

The long and flexible branches of Dutchman's pipe enable its propagation by means of serpentine layering.

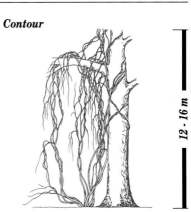

Contour

12 - 16 m

A flowering branch

*The unusual shape of the flowers
is part of a complicated
mechanism that serves to prevent
self-pollination: some insect
species involuntarily become
short-term prisoners.*

Cultivation

also tolerates shade very well. The more sunshine the plant gets, the more its moisture requirements increase. Moisture apart, Dutchman's pipe has no special demands and grows in any kind of common soil. It also tolerates cooler climatic conditions and it can be grown at sheltered sites up to temperature zone D.

The soil should contain sufficient moisture and be watered adequately during lengthy dry spells. Dutchman's pipe can be planted either in spring or in autumn. The young plants should be covered with leaves and green brushwood for the winter. Dutchman's pipe tolerates both autumn and spring pruning very well.

Lesser Bougainvillea
Bougainvillea glabra

This is a most attractive climber reaching a height of about 4-5 m. Its flowers are tiny but they have large, impressively coloured bracts. The whole then looks like one large flower which is red, pink, white or dark violet, depending on the cultivar. The flower clusters adorn the plant throughout the summer, till autumn. Lesser bougainvillea is native to South America where it grows wild in Peru and Brazil.

This genus was named after French navigator Louis Antoine de Bougainville (1729-1811) who sailed around the world in 1766-1769. The biggest of the Solomon Islands was also named after him.

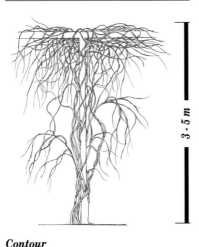

Contour

Use

The plant is suitable for pergolas and sunny walls. It also looks very beautiful on columns and on bare trunks. It also grows well in pots and it is even cultivated as an indoor plant.

Site

The plant is very demanding as to site and in Europe can be grown only in the warmest regions in temperature zone A. For instance, it is grown a lot on the Mediterranean. It is less demanding as far as soil is concerned and does not mind common garden soil, which, however, must not be too dry.

Cultivation

Its cultivation does not require any special care, apart from adequate watering during lengthy dry spells. Sometimes it is also possible to train the plant by pruning.

3 - 5 m

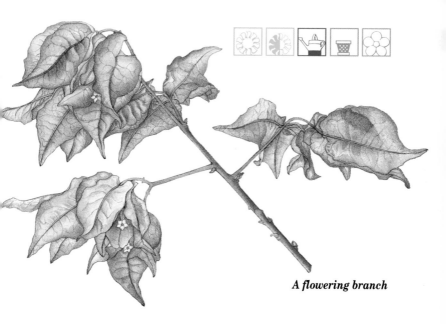

A flowering branch

Bougainvillea is also well known as an indoor plant. It cannot reach larger sizes when raised in pots, but it can also be grown outdoors, on balconies and terraces in large tubs. In cooler regions it must, however, be moved into frost-free rooms for the winter. The most suitable temperature for overwintering the plants in pots is around 5 °C.

Large pots with water reservoirs are used for cultivating climbing plants in pots: a - substratum, b - filtration layer, c - water reservoir, d - overflow for superfluous water, e - discharge opening.

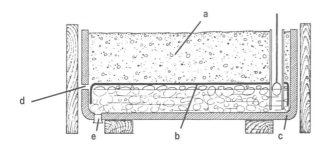

Oriental Bittersweet

Celastrus orbiculatus

This plant is native to Japan and China where it grows in Yunnan and Szechwan. The dioecious flowers of oriental bittersweet are tiny, green and inconspicuous. Its fruits, which remain on the branches till late in winter, are much more ornamental. They are dark yellow three-chambered capsules which split to reveal shining scarlet seeds. For oriental bittersweet to bear fruit there should be at least two specimens of different sexes grown next to each other. The golden-yellow colours of the leaves in autumn is also attractive.

Use

Oriental bittersweet has many uses. It is quite suitable for large pergolas, the walls of large buildings and columns and poles. It also quickly overgrows fences, screening them from view. It also creeps along the trunks of old trees. But it should never be used for young trees and it should not be allowed to twist itself around gutter pipes either. Growing along a support, oriental bittersweet twists very tightly around it and thickens quickly. Then it literally strangles the trunks of young trees and crushes gutter pipes. For that reason it is called *Baumwürger* (tree strangler) in German. Attractive yellow and red fruited branches are suitable for use in dried flower arrangements.

A flowering branch

Site

The plant likes sunshine but also tolerates partial shade. It grows very vigorously in any kind of common garden soil and can also be grown in poor quality soil, as long as it is not too dry. Oriental bittersweet tolerates severe frost. It can be grown in the coolest temperature zone.

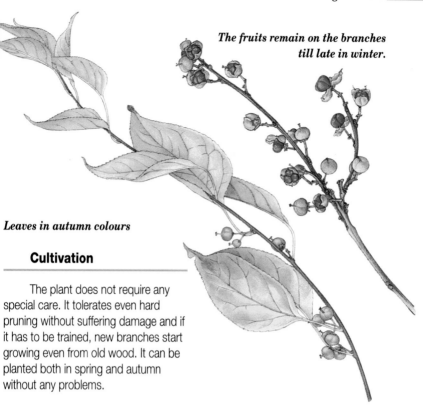

The fruits remain on the branches till late in winter.

Leaves in autumn colours

Cultivation

The plant does not require any special care. It tolerates even hard pruning without suffering damage and if it has to be trained, new branches start growing even from old wood. It can be planted both in spring and autumn without any problems.

Contour

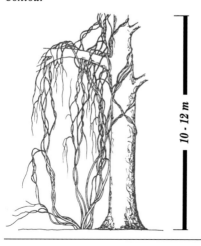

10 - 12 m

Oriental bittersweet is dangerous to gutter pipes as it is able to crush them completely.

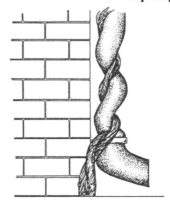

Silver Fleece Vine

Fallopia baldschuanicum

This quite modest liana is native to the former khanate of Baldshuan, a region of Tibet. It grows very vigorously and forms a huge mass. It really grows with rocket speed - after pruning new branches may reach as much as 6 m within a year. The flowers of silver fleece vine are very tiny and are arranged in large, dense racemes. Later they slowly change into similar-looking fruit branches and turn the whole plant into a large white mass in summer.

Use and site

The plant is quite suitable for pergolas and walls but only for large ones. It also looks well on noise barriers and old trees which it completely covers after a while. It can also be grown on fences but in this case it should be pruned regularly, otherwise it will literally crush the fence.

Silver fleece vine has no special site requirements appart from sufficient light. It grows almost everywhere with the exception of full shade - which it does not tolerate. Fleece vine also grows in colder regions and it can be planted in temperature zone E. In warmer regions it also grows well in pots, but it overwinters badly in pots in cooler regions.

Support plates holding a lattice away from the wall should enable quick runoff of water.

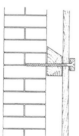

A thin lattice of strong battens is suitable as a support.

A flowering branch of silver fleece vine

Cultivation

It does not require any special care. During excessive drought, watering is useful but not necessary. Therefore care should be focused particularly on occasionally pruning the plants to remove excessive mass. The plants should also be rejuvenated by hard pruning now and then.

Fallopia aubertii is another widely cultivated species. The two species are very similar and they are often confused. They also have the same demands and use. *Fallopia aubertii* differs in having pure white flowers without a pink tinge and flower peduncles covered with fine hairs (the peduncles of silver fleece vine are glabrous). *Fallopia aubertii* grows somewhat less vigorously. Apart from the more recent Latin name *Fallopia*, the older name *Polygonum* is also often used.

Contour

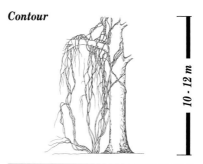

10 - 12 m

Brown's Honeysuckle

Lonicera x *brownii*

Honeysuckles were given their Latin name
in honour of Adam Lonicer, a Frankfurt physician and
botanist (1528-1586). The majority of the approximately
200 species of this genus are both deciduous and
evergreen shrubs and only a minority of them are
climbers. They do not reach any very big size - and
Brown's honeysuckle is one of the smallest among
them, only three metres high. It is particularly
remarkable for its scarlet flowers which form in great
numbers from May till August and later develop into
round, glossy red fruit. The 'Dropmore Scarlet' cultivar,
one of the most beautiful, does not come into flower
until June but flowers till October.

Use

Brown's honeysuckle is the result
of crossing two North American species
- *Lonicera sempervirens* and *Lonicera
hirsutum*. It is quite suitable for fences,
rails, pergolas or low retaining walls. It is
too small to be used for larger buildings
and supports.

*The majority of
climbers should be
tied to temporary
supports after they
are planted.*

Site and cultivation

The plant is undemanding and
grows in any kind of common soil, as
long as it is not too dry. It grows well
both in sunshine and partial shade.
Brown's honeysuckle can be grown in
cooler regions, it also overwinters well in
temperature zone D.

It does not require any special
care, apart from watering during long
spells of drought. Its seedlings can be
planted both in spring and autumn and
after planting the branches should be
tied to their support. It is advisable to
prune the branches after flowering. This
will promote branching and prevent
later denudation of the lower parts of
the shrub. The plants should be treated
with special substances to protect them
from aphids, which often like to attack
the young branches.

A *flowering branch*

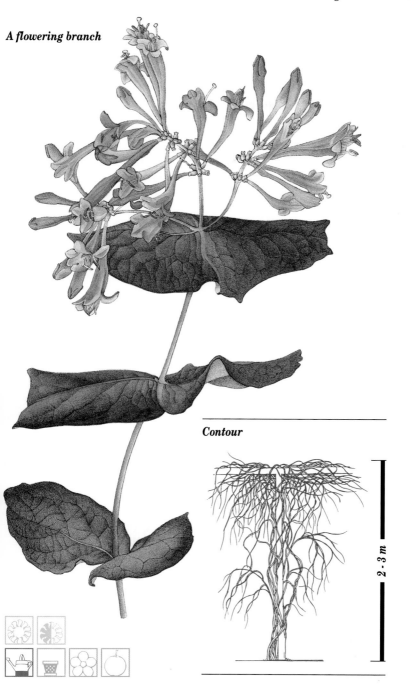

Contour

2 - 3 m

Everflowering Honeysuckle

Lonicera x *heckrottii*

It is a less vigorously growing honeysuckle and reaches a maximum height of three metres. It does not twine tightly around its support and the new branches need to be trained to the support now and then. The flowers with a length of up to 5 cm are the greatest attraction of this plant and are said to be the most beautiful of all honeysuckles. The plant blooms profusely from June till October and its red and yellow flowers have a very pleasant scent. After flowering, its branches are adorned with round, purplish-red fruit.

Site and use

Everflowering honeysuckle is very hardy and can be grown in cooler regions - it even tolerates the frosts of temperature zone E well. It is quite suitable for fences, rails, pergolas and low retaining walls.

Cultivation

Everflowering honeysuckle is capable of surviving a period of drought better than any other honeysuckle species. Its seedlings can be planted either in spring or in autumn, shoots should be tied to their support and cut back after planting, which will promote branching and prevent later denudation of the lower parts of the shrub. After flowering thin the whole shrub and remove weak and broken branches and old drying branches. The plants should be treated with special substances to protect them from aphids, which often like to attack the young shoots.

Contour

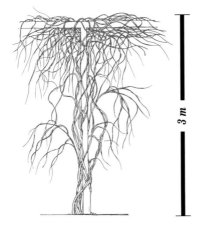

3 m

A flowering branch

Henry Honeysuckle

Lonicera henryi

It differs very significantly from other honeysuckle species by its robust growth, its foliage and its flowers. It can reach a height of 6 metres and grows quite vigorously. The flowers of the majority of honeysuckle species are their greatest attraction. However, the flowers of Henry honeysuckle are quite inconspicuous and are insignificant as ornamental flowers. This species is cultivated in particular because it is one of a small number of climbing plants that are evergreen.

A fertile branch

Use

It is quite suitable for fences, screening them perfectly from view, and for rails, columns and bare trunks. It is a somewhat faster grower than other climbing honeysuckles and so it also does well on larger pergolas and retaining walls. It looks well on the edge of a terrace, from which it may hang down.

Site

Henry honeysuckle grows in any kind of common soil, as long as it is not too dry. It prefers partial shade but also grows very well in shade. It does not tolerate winter sunshine, which damages its leaves at low temperatures. Henry honeysuckle is quite heat-loving and can be grown only in grape-growing regions.

A flowering branch

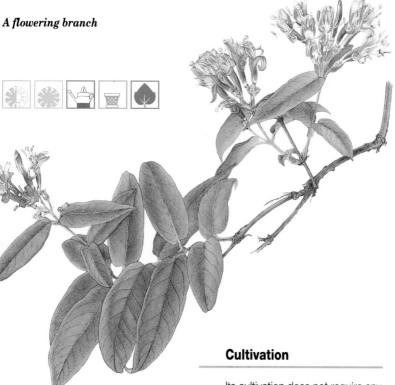

Cultivation

Its cultivation does not require any special care apart from watering during lengthy dry spells. The seedlings should preferably be planted in spring to enable them to root well before winter. After planting, the shoots should be tied to their support. In cooler regions it is advisable to cover the young plants with green brushwood for the winter.

The majority of climbing plants do not like to hang down. Branches which do not find a support and bend down try to bend up again at their ends, and if this effort is futile they stop growing. Henry honeysuckle is one of the few exceptions in this respect - it can be planted above a retaining wall and allowed to hang down.

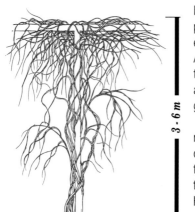

3 - 6 m

Contour

Japanese Honeysuckle

Lonicera japonica

This is a small species reaching a height of only about 2-3 metres. Its flowers are quite inconspicuous, white at first and giving way to yellow as they fade. They are remarkable for their pleasant strong scent. The small black fruit is insignificant as well. The leaves are tiny, light green and in the 'Reticulata' cultivar they are yellow marbled. Japanese honeysuckle is native to East Asia where it grows wild in Japan, China, Korea and in Taiwan.

A flowering branch of the original species with green leaves

It is particularly the cultivar 'Reticulata' which is grown for its beautiful leaves. Young branches have ovate leaves, and later leaves with several sinuate-toothed lobes. The leaves remain on the plant for very long - often till spring.

Use

The plant is quite suitable for fences, screening them from view, for rails, pergolas or low retaining walls. It is too small to be used for larger structures. This is another honeysuckle species can be planted above retaining walls and allowed to hang down.

Site

Japanese honeysuckle grows in any kind of common soil, as long as it is not too dry. It prefers partial shade but also grows well in the sunshine. In sheltered sites, Japanese honeysuckle can be planted up to temperature zone D.

A leaf of an older plant

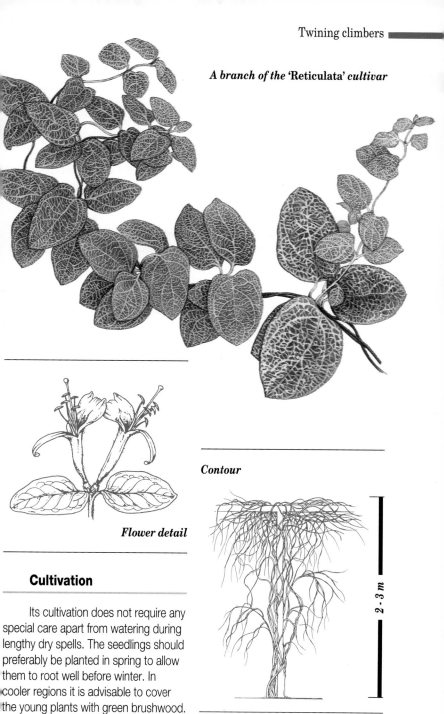

A branch of the 'Reticulata' *cultivar*

Flower detail

Contour

2 - 3 m

Cultivation

Its cultivation does not require any special care apart from watering during lengthy dry spells. The seedlings should preferably be planted in spring to allow them to root well before winter. In cooler regions it is advisable to cover the young plants with green brushwood.

Tellman's honeysuckle

Lonicera x *tellmanniana*

This species was derived in Budapest (Hungary) in 1920 by crossing the North American *Lonicera sempervirens* and the Chinese *Lonicera tragophylla*. Although it is one of the most robust climbing honeysuckles it is not a very vigorous climber. It is remarkable particularly for its beautiful flowers which are produced in large numbers from May till June and sometimes again in autumn. Later the flowers turn into round, glossy, red fruits.

Use

This species is quite suitable for fences, rails, columns and bare trunks. It is a somewhat faster grower than other climbing honeysuckles and therefore Tellman's honeysuckle also does well on larger pergolas and walls. Its fruit serves as food for birds in autumn and winter.

Site

The plant grows in any kind of common soil, as long as it is not too dry. It prefers partial shade but it also grows in sunshine and tolerates shade as well. In sheltered places, Tellman's honeysuckle can be planted up to temperature zone D.

Cultivation

Water during lengthy dry spells. The seedlings can be planted either in spring or in autumn and after planting the branches should be tied to a support. It is advisable to cut back branches that are past flowering. This will promote branching and prevent a denudation of the lower parts of the shrub. Beware of aphids! As almost all honeysuckles, this species is also

Contour

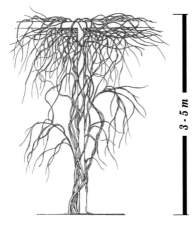

3 - 5 m

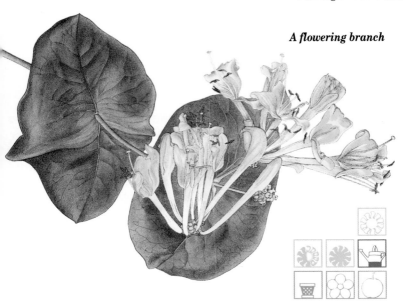

A flowering branch

often attacked by aphids. When aphids appear, the plants should be sprayed with special protective substances. The plants are able to resist aphids better in soils containing sufficient moisture.

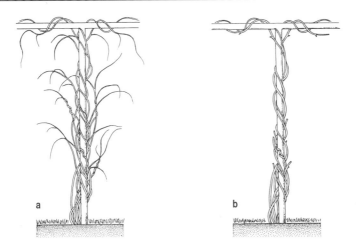

a

b

Removal of weak, dry or damaged branches and thinning of the whole shrub, is beneficial to honeysuckles. a - a shrub before pruning, b - after pruning.

Common Moonseed

Menispermum canadense

As suggested by its Latin name, this plant is native to the North American continent, where it grows in river valleys and on the edge of forests from Ontario to Manitoba down to Arkansas in the south. It is a twining climber which can reach a height of 5 metres. It is cultivated for its beautiful foliage which is able to form a dense and vivid green cover on a suitable support.

An inconspicuous greenish flower cluster of common moonseed

The plant's tiny, yellow-green flowers are arranged in small inconspicuous racemes, concealed in great part amidst the dense foliage. The fruits, which form miniature bunches of black berries remindful of grapes, are somewhat more attractive.

The fruits, or rather the seeds hidden in them, have given the whole genus its scientific name, as well as its names in a number of other languages. The scientific name is composed of two Greek words: *"mene"* means "moon" and *"sperma"* is "seed". Thus the name expresses the seed shape which reminds one of a crescent. The fruits are inedible and poisonous.

Use

The plant is quite suitable for pergolas, walls and old trees. It also quickly covers fences, screening them from view. Its fruit provides food for birds.

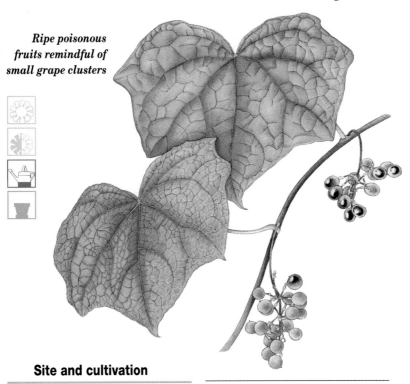

Ripe poisonous fruits remindful of small grape clusters

Site and cultivation

Common moonseed has minimum site requirements. It grows in any kind of soil with a sufficient moisture content. It likes partial shade but also grows well in sunshine. It tolerates cooler climates and can easily be grown in temperature zone D.

This species does not require any special care apart from watering during lengthy dry spells. Its seedlings can be planted either in spring or in autumn and after planting, the shoots should be tied to a support.

Menispermum dauricum is a species very similar to common moonseed. It is native to Central Siberia, China and Japan and differs from the previous species only in small

Contour

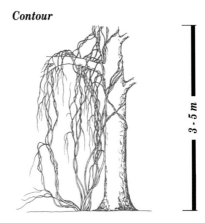

3 - 5 m

details (e.g. the pubescence). Its demands and use are also the same as for common moonseed.

Grecian Silk Vine

Periploca graeca

This deciduous climber is native to southern Europe and Asia Minor. It is striking because of its deep green and glossy foliage which does not change colour even in autumn when the leaves are shed. The plant bears clusters of 4-12 flowers, which are also interesting. They are yellow-green outside and violet-brown inside. In summer the flower clusters cover the plant in large numbers. Slender fruits, about 10-12 cm long, hide a great quantity of downy seeds.

Contour

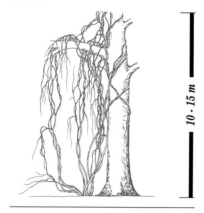

10 - 15 m

Site

This plant requires humus-rich soil with a sufficient moisture content, and sunshine or partial shade. Before planting, it is advisable to enrich the soil with compost. Grecian silk vine is heat-loving and outside grape-growing regions it can be grown only exceptionally, in sheltered places.

Cultivation

It is advisable to keep the soil sufficiently moist and to water if necessary. If Grecian silk vine is partly damaged by frost or if it spreads too much it can be pruned as required. It tolerates pruning very well.

Older specimens are fully hardy in the temperature zones indicated but young plants should be covered with leaves and green brushwood for the winter. The seedlings should preferably be planted in spring.

Use

Grecian silk vine is a fast-growing species. It is quite suitable for large pergolas, walls, big supports, columns and poles. It quickly covers fences, screening them well from view. It also creeps along old tree trunks.

*A flowering branch
and a flower detail*

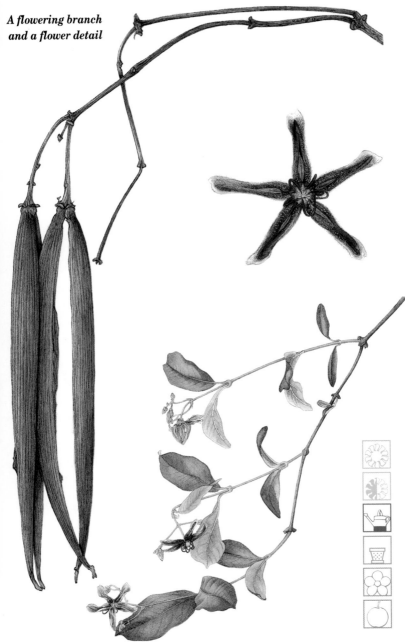

The fruits always grow in pairs

Chinese Silk Vine

Periploca sepium

This silk vine is also a deciduous climber, but it is native to northern China and reaches a height of about 10 metres. It is striking because of its deep green and glossy foliage which turns yellow in autumn. Unlike the previous species, Chinese silk vine has smaller and less impressive flowers and harder fruits which split after they ripen and release a great quantity of downy seeds.

Use

Chinese silk vine grows very fast and when it is damaged by frost in colder regions it will grow profusely again in spring. It is quite suitable for large pergolas, walls, columns, poles or fences and it screens them well from view. It also creeps along old tree trunks.

Split fruits with seeds

Site

Unlike the previous species it is able to survive in any kind of common soil with a sufficient moisture content. It grows both in sunshine and partial shade. Chinese silk vine is heat-loving and outside grape-growing regions it can be grown only exceptionally, in sheltered places.

Cultivation

If the plants are partly damaged by frost or spread too much they can be pruned as required. They tolerate pruning very well and will grow

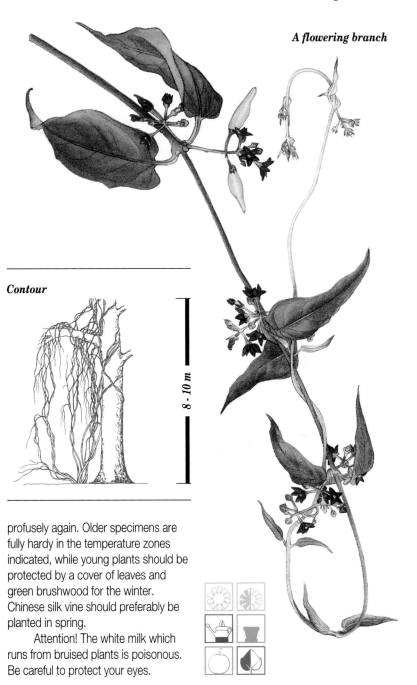

A flowering branch

Contour

8 - 10 m

profusely again. Older specimens are fully hardy in the temperature zones indicated, while young plants should be protected by a cover of leaves and green brushwood for the winter. Chinese silk vine should preferably be planted in spring.

Attention! The white milk which runs from bruised plants is poisonous. Be careful to protect your eyes.

Chinese Schizandra

Schisandra chinensis

This species is a quite vigorously growing twining climber which can reach a height of 10 metres. Its large pinkish flowers have a pleasant scent and a diameter of approximately 1.5 cm. They flower from May till June. They are quite inconspicuous, however, and, hidden under the leaves, they are not easily spotted. The scarlet fruits similar to cherries are more interesting than the flowers. The smooth, deep green leaves, which are up to 12 cm long and turn yellow in autumn, also contribute to its striking effect.

Use and site

Schizandra is quite suitable for pergolas, retaining walls and walls. It also grows very well along columns, poles and old trees.

In Russia, Chinese schizandra is called "Chinese lemon". This name reflects both the high vitamin C content in the fruits and a pleasant lemon-like scent that can be smelled when the plant is bruised. Apart from vitamin C, schizandra also contains certain stimulants. It stimulates the activity of the human body when nerves are exhausted and is used as a medicine for stress and colds.

It is quite hardy and can be grown in temperature zone D. In winter it tolerates temperatures below -20 °C without suffering damage. Problems arise in maritime climates in spring when the plants start budding too early. Then late spring frosts usually burn the newly sprouted branches. Although the

The fruits contain large quantities of vitamin C. In Russia soft drinks are made from them and the plant is grown on plantations.

A flowering branch

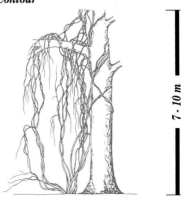

plant will usually grow again without problems, it does not flower any more.

Cultivation

When cultivating schizandra it is necessary first of all to keep the soil sufficiently moist, which is very important. Apart from that, the plant does not require any special care. Older plants are hardy in the temperature zones indicated but late spring frosts damage early buds. Young plants should be protected with a cover of leaves and green brushwood for the winter. Planting should preferably be carried out in spring.

Contour

7 - 10 m

73

Regel's Tripterygium

Tripterygium regelii

This modest twining climber native to Japan and Korea could have many uses. However, in Europe it is still almost unknown and there it is grown only in a few arboretums or botanical gardens. Its tiny flowers (with a diameter of approximately 8 mm) are yellow-white and are arranged in panicles that can reach a length of 25 cm. The fruits are green-white nuts with three wings and measure about 2 cm. The pale green leaves may be over 20 cm long.

Use

The plant is quite suitable for covering large pergolas, the walls of large buildings and columns, poles and old tree trunks. It can also be grown without a support and then it may form a 2-metre high hemispherical shrub.

Under favourable conditions, flowers turn into three-winged nuts which have given this species its scientific name (tri = three, pteris = wing).

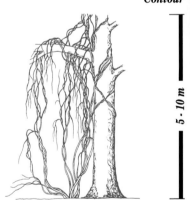

Contour

5 - 10 m

Site

This plant grows very well in partial shade and does not mind sunshine either. It grows vigorously in any kind of common garden soil, as long as it is not too dry. It is quite heat-loving and can be grown only in warmer regions (temperature zone C and warmer zones).

A flowering branch

Cultivation

Its cultivation does not require any special care. The plant tolerates even hard pruning without suffering damage and if it is necessary to train it, it grows quite well from old wood as well. Its new, vigorously growing branches easily reach a length of more than 2 metres after regenerative pruning.

Getting a plant seedling may not be easy as this species is not commonly cultivated in ornamental nurseries at present.

Chinese Wisteria

Wisteria sinensis

This is one of the most beautiful climbing plants. Its flowers, arranged in splendid clusters up to 30 cm long, are the plant's greatest attraction. They flower from April till May and on rare occasions still appear in July. The plant was named in honour of Kaspar Wistar, the American natural historian (1761-1818). Chinese wisteria is native to China, as its name suggests.

Use

Chinese wisteria is especially suitable for pergolas and walls exposed to sunshine. It also looks well on columns and on bare trunks. When choosing a site you should remember that wisteria is quite a robust plant.

Contour

15 - 20 m

Long fruits develop from some flowers late in summer.

Site

The plant requires a site fully exposed to sunshine, with good soil rich in humus and moisture. Nevertheless, it does not like excessive moisture and therefore a hole prepared for it should be quite deep (80 cm) and the bottom should be covered with gravel. Wisteria is heat-loving and can only be cultivated in temperature zone C and warmer zones.

Cultivars include white forms and forms with double flowers.

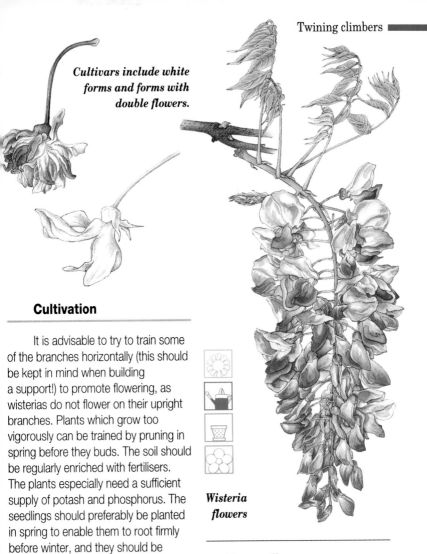

Cultivation

It is advisable to try to train some of the branches horizontally (this should be kept in mind when building a support!) to promote flowering, as wisterias do not flower on their upright branches. Plants which grow too vigorously can be trained by pruning in spring before they buds. The soil should be regularly enriched with fertilisers. The plants especially need a sufficient supply of potash and phosphorus. The seedlings should preferably be planted in spring to enable them to root firmly before winter, and they should be shaded after planting.

Wisteria floribunda is a species related to Chinese wisteria. Its growth is lower (usually only up to 5 m), but its flower clusters are even longer than those of Chinese wisteria and may reach a length of 90 cm in the *Wisteria floribunda* cultivar called 'Macrobotrys'! *Wisteria floribunda* it has the same demands as the previous species.

Wisteria flowers

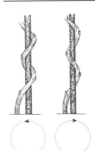

Chinese wisteria (left) may also be distinguished from the very similar **Wisteria floribunda** *(right) by the direction in which it twines.*

Tendril climbers

Tendril climbers form specialised organs (tendrils) to cling to their supports. These tendrils are modified leaves or branches. However, not even these highly specialised organs are able to "catch hold of" a bare wall, and they need a support.

Supports

A support must be thin enough for the tendrils to twist around them (to "grasp" them). Therefore metal screens or nets are very suitable material. To provide the necessary protection from corrosion, plastic-coated metal netting is almost ideal and is practically indestructible even if it is not painted.

Removable parts of a support allow access to places covered by plants.

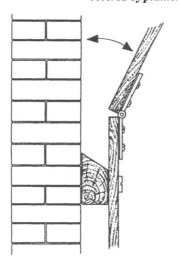

Good-quality screens with durable anti-corrosion layers produced for this purpose by specialised firms are available. For more robust species, for instance for some vines (Vitis), it is also possible to use trellises made of battens with cross-sections not exceeding 20x30 mm. Suitable mesh sizes are from 100x100 up to 200x200 mm. The wood must be treated with a wood preservative. Screens and nets for tendril climbers can be fixed closer to a wall - 30-50 mm is sufficient. A larger distance is perfectly all right.

Use of tendril climbers

Tendril climbers are particularly suitable for covering wall surfaces because they spread laterally. They can be used for covering surfaces between windows and in all places where a plant cover should be prevented from spreading outside a surface area limited by a support. The cost of buying a support will pay itself back in the form of easier maintenance as it will not be necessary to trim the plant cover. Removable supports will even make it possible to cover those spots to which access is required from time to time.

The well-loved clematis uses the rachises of the pinnate leaves as tendrils.

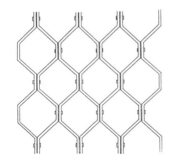

A clematis flower

A metal support made of thin bars (left), netting (right).

Monkshood Vine

Ampelopsis aconitifolia

This species is native to the north of China and to Mongolia and is closely related to Vitis. Its leaves are deeply incised and very fine, and the whole plant really looks quite nice and airy. Unlike Vitis and Parthenocissus, the leaves of Ampelopsis usually do not turn such a fine colour in autumn, which may be why these plants are not as popular. The tiny green flowers are inconspicuous. In Europe the fruits ripen only in warmer regions. Their colour may shade from yellow to orange or even brownish. They are arranged in small, meager racemes.

Use

Monkshood vine is a fast-growing climber. It is quite suitable for pergolas, retaining walls and walls. It twines well over fences forming dense but finely structured plant covers along them. It is also useful to cover columns or slopes. Sometimes it does not do well on old trees.

Site and cultivation

This plant grows best in the sunshine but does not mind partial shade. It grows very well in any kind of common garden soil and also tolerates dry and permeable soils. It is a hardy plant and can also be grown in cooler regions, it also withstands the frosts of temperature zone D quite well. It should not be planted where wasps visiting its flowers would be objectionable.

Its cultivation does not require any special care. In case that it spreads too much it can be pruned as required any time. It does not mind a pruning of its old wood either and after hard pruning it will grow vigorously again. Older specimens are fully hardy in the temperature zones indicated but young plants should be protected by a cover of leaves and green brushwood for the winter. The seedlings should preferably be planted in spring.

Contour

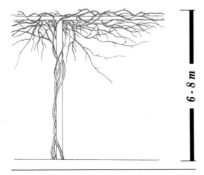

6 - 8 m

A branch with tendrils

Spikenard Ampelopsis

Ampelopsis megalophylla

This is another of the approximately 20 ampelopsis species. It is native to the west of China. It looks quite different from the previous species, which has a fine structure. Spikenard ampelopsis has huge, bipinnate leaves which can reach a size of half a meter. They turn yellow-red in autumn although this is not typical of the Ampelopsis genus. The branches are glabrous, strong and have large buds. The tiny green flowers are inconspicuous. The fruits are about 8 mm in diameter and ripen in meager racemes, but only in warm regions. They are purple at first and shade into black later. They are said to be edible.

Use

In favourable climatic conditions where it is not damaged by frost in winter, this plant is a very fast-growing climber. It is quite suitable for large pergolas, retaining walls and walls. Its fruit is a favourite bird food in winter.

Cultivation

Its cultivation does not require any special care apart from watering during lengthy dry spells. Older specimens are fully hardy in the temperature zones indicated but young plants should be protected by a cover of leaves and green brushwood for the winter. The seedlings are best planted in spring. After planting, the branches should be tied to a support.

Site

Spikenard ampelopsis is a modest species. It prefers sunshine but does not mind partial shade. It grows well in any kind of common garden soil but does better in loamy soils than in sandy ones. It grows reliably only in the warmest temperature

Contour

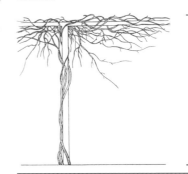

6 - 10 m

A branch of spikenard ampelopsis

zones, A and B. In sheltered places and given a winter cover of green brushwood it can also be grown in temperature zone C (the limit for grape cultivation).

Ampelopsis brevipedunculata is the third ampelopsis species cultivated. It has tiny leaves and its chief interest lies in its fruits, which are green when they start to ripen, then turn violet-blue and finally clear amethyst with dark dots. There may be fruits of different colours on the plant simultaneously. This species has similar requirements to spikenard ampelopsis.

A fully developed leaf

Horticultural varieties of clematis

Clematis x hybrida

They are the most beautiful and best-known climbers cultivated in the garden. Usually, they do not grow as big as some original species and they are not suitable for covering large surfaces. But their flowers are remarkable for their extraordinary beauty and they often flower so lushly that the leaves are completely hidden behind them. Moreover, the flowers provide nectar for bees. Because of their conspicuousness and demanding character clematis are typical solitary plants.

Clematis classification

Clematises may be classified into three groups according to the period of flowering:

1st group: plants flowering from May till June, and faintly until September. Flowers are formed on the short branches growing from the previous year's wood. Cultivars 'Lasurstern', 'Nelly Moser'.

Clematis cultivar flowering in purple

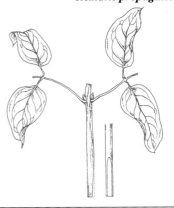

Correct preparation of a cutting for clematis propagation

A flowering branch of a horticultural variety of clematis

2nd group: plants coming into flower at the end of June and in July, and continuing to flower to some extent until October. In this group too, flowers appear on the short branches growing from the previous year's wood. However, unlike the first group, new branches, on which a smaller number of flowers blossom continuously till autumn, develop simultaneously. Cultivars 'Blue Gem', 'Lady Northeliff', 'Marie Boisselot'.

3rd group: plants flowering from the end of July till September and October. Flowers develop on new branches (annual shoots). Cultivars 'Gipsy Queen', 'Ville de Lyon', *Clematis* x *jackmanii*.

Contour

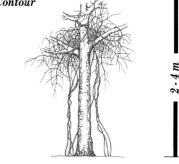

2 - 4 m

Use and site

Clematis are quite suitable for arches over gates, for pergolas, retaining walls and walls and they also look well on columns and poles. They are typical solitary plants and are suitable for the best situations in a well-maintained garden.

These plants need sufficient sunshine but at the same time they do not tolerate scorching heat. South walls unprotected from the midday heat are quite unsuitable. The root necks of clematis are especially delicate and therefore the lower parts of the plant should be shaded. To this end it is advisable to plant perennials or low shrubs in front of clematis, and at fences the needed shade can be provided by the concrete base of the fence. Before planting, it is advisable to dig a large hole (at least 70 cm deep), to cover the bottom with gravel and to fill it with good soil mixed with compost and crushed old plaster or ground limestone. Clematis does not tolerate acidic soil with a pH below 6. If clematis are covered during the winter they can also be grown in the very harsh climate of zone E.

Cultivation

Clematis should be regularly treated with mixed fertilisers (see on burning bush). Sufficient moisture should be provided by watering especially near walls. In cooler regions, you should shovel leaves around the plants for the winter. The leaves should then be covered with green brushwood to prevent them from being blown away by the wind. The seedlings should be planted in spring in such a way that the point for grafting is approximately 5 cm deep and branches should be trimmed to 5-7 buds.

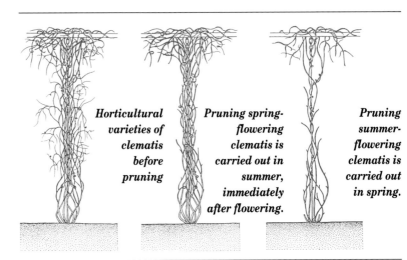

Horticultural varieties of clematis before pruning

Pruning spring-flowering clematis is carried out in summer, immediately after flowering.

Pruning summer-flowering clematis is carried out in spring.

The cultivars belonging to the first group should not be pruned very often. If pruning is necessary now and then it should never be done in spring or autumn as that would damage the flowering branches. In principle, the plants should be pruned immediately after flowering, in June, to enable the development of new branches by autumn, which will make sure the plants flower the following year. The plants of the second group need not be pruned either. However, pruning in early spring may be useful as after such pruning the main period of flowering is delayed and shifted to the later summer months. The clematis of the third group flower on their new branches and hard spring pruning promotes the growth of new branches and thus also the development of flowers.

Examples of horticultural varieties of clematis cultivars

Anemone Clematis

Clematis montana

Anemone clematis is an original botanical species. It is native to the Himalayas of central and western China where it grows at altitudes from 1800 up to 4000 m. It is more robust and taller than large-flowered hybrids. Therefore it is also suitable for covering larger areas. Its mostly white and sometimes pink flowers do not grow so big but this does not make them less impressive. From May till June they flower on the short branches growing from the previous year's wood. They have a slight vanilla scent.

Use

This species is quite suitable for fences (especially for arches over gates), pergolas, retaining walls and walls, columns and poles. It can also be grown with success in pots on terraces and balconies. Its flowers provide nectar for bees.

The original species has white flowers.

Site and cultivation

This plant has more modest requirements than hybrid clematis as to its site and especially the soil. It will do with a common kind of garden soil which is not too acidic and contains calcium. Before planting, the soil should be enriched with ground limestone or crushed old plaster. This clematis grows both in sunshine and partial shade. Its root necks are sensitive to scorching heat and therefore the lower parts of the plant should be shaded. To this end, it is advisable to plant perennials or low shrubs in front of anemone clematis, and at fences the required shade can also be provided by the concrete base of the fence. Anemone clematis tolerates severe frosts. It can be grown in the coolest temperature zone F.

The soil should occasionally be enriched with mixed fertilisers or with manure. The soil should contain

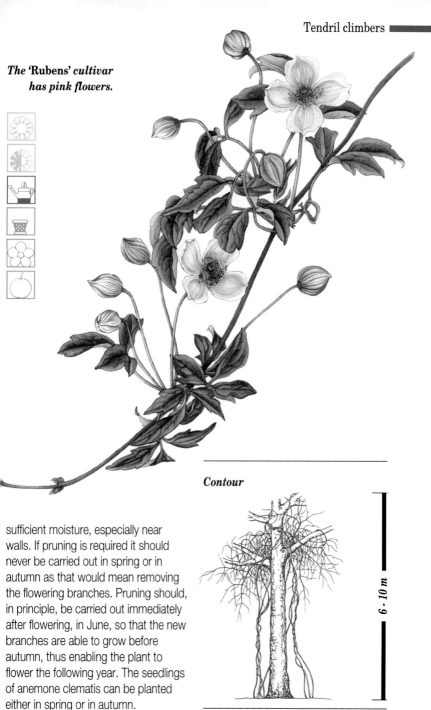

*The 'Rubens' cultivar
has pink flowers.*

Contour

6 - 10 m

sufficient moisture, especially near walls. If pruning is required it should never be carried out in spring or in autumn as that would mean removing the flowering branches. Pruning should, in principle, be carried out immediately after flowering, in June, so that the new branches are able to grow before autumn, thus enabling the plant to flower the following year. The seedlings of anemone clematis can be planted either in spring or in autumn.

Golden Clematis

Clematis tangutica

This is also an original botanical species which is more robust and taller than large-flowered hybrids. The main flowering period is in June, when tiny yellow flowers develop in large numbers. Later on, until autumn, flowers continue to develop, but in fewer numbers. The silvery down on the fruits is also decorative. Golden clematis is native to Mongolia and northwestern China.

Use

Golden clematis is very vigorous even under average conditions and grows very fast. It is quite suitable for arches over gates, pergolas, retaining walls and walls. It also looks very well on columns and poles. It has also been grown with success in pots on terraces and balconies. Its flowers provide nectar for bees.

Site

The plant is very modest. It does not do well in soils that are too acidic and do not contain sufficient calcium. Therefore the soil should be enriched with ground limestone or crushed old plaster before planting. Its root necks are sensitive to scorching heat and therefore the lower parts of the plant should be shaded by planting

Silvery flower clusters of botanical clematis

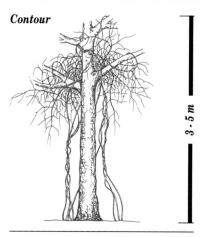

Contour

3 - 5 m

Golden clematis

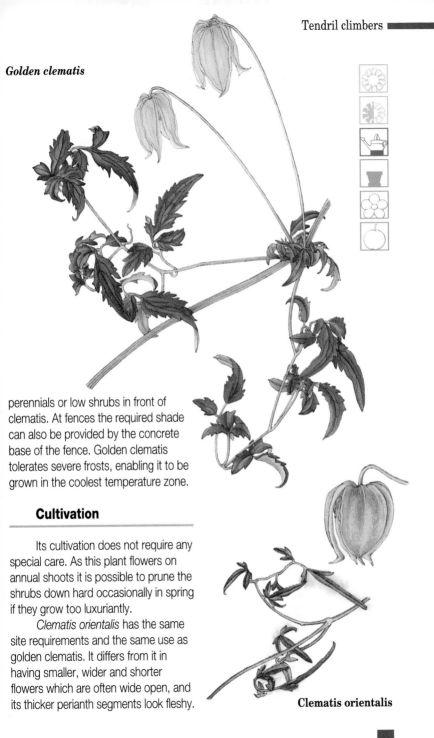

perennials or low shrubs in front of clematis. At fences the required shade can also be provided by the concrete base of the fence. Golden clematis tolerates severe frosts, enabling it to be grown in the coolest temperature zone.

Cultivation

Its cultivation does not require any special care. As this plant flowers on annual shoots it is possible to prune the shrubs down hard occasionally in spring if they grow too luxuriantly.

Clematis orientalis has the same site requirements and the same use as golden clematis. It differs from it in having smaller, wider and shorter flowers which are often wide open, and its thicker perianth segments look fleshy.

Clematis orientalis

Bluecrown Passionflower

Passiflora coerulea

Since time immemorial the exotic flowers of this very attractive climber have been regarded as the symbols of the Crucifixion - nails and a thorny crown. This also accounts for the plant's scientific name (Latin *passio* = suffering, *flos* = flower). Another of the attractions of bluecrown passionflower are its fruits which when ripe are egg-shaped and of an orange colour.

Use

The plant grows very lushly but does not grow very big. It is especially suitable for sunny walls. It splendidly in pots (it is often cultivated as an indoor plant). The potted plants should be overwintered at a temperature around 5 °C. The fruits of bluecrown passionflower are edible but other species are cultivated especially for their fruits.

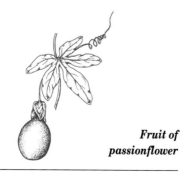

Fruit of passionflower

Site and cultivation

Passionflower requires a warm and sheltered site, preferably in full sunshine or in partial shade. The plant does not like sites that are too dry or too wet. It is very heat-loving and can only be cultivated in the warmest regions of Europe, in temperature zones A and B.

It is advisable to keep the soil sufficiently moist and to water the plant as required. If the plant is damaged by frost or if it spreads too much, it can be pruned as required. Not even older specimens are fully hardy and the parts of the plant that are above ground may easily be damaged by severe frosts. Therefore the lower parts of the plant should be protected by a cover of straw and green brushwood for the winter and the plant should be covered up as high as possible. Planting is best done in spring.

Flowering passionflower

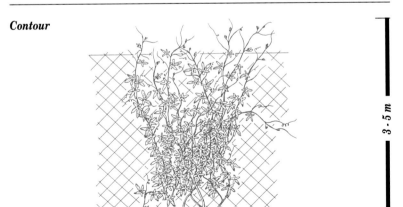

Contour

3 - 5 m

Bristly Greenbrier

Smilax hispida

This is a modest North American climber with broad, ovate, smooth leaves 10 to 15 cm long. The leaves are parallel-veined, which is typical of all monocotyledonous plants (bristly greenbrier belongs to the lily family). The globose flower clusters consist of as many as 25 inconspicuous tiny greenish flowers. The lushly growing branches have quite tiny tendrils and thin small spines. In spite of its attractiveness and modest demands, bristly greenbrier is cultivated very rarely.

The genus includes over 300 species. Most of them grow in the tropical regions of both hemispheres. *Smilax rotundifolia*, which has similar uses and demands as bristly greenbrier, is also native to the North American continent. The roots of some tropical species have pharmaceutical applications, as for instance sarsaparilla. Sarsaparilla is used for treating rheumatism and skin complaints, and as an auxiliary medicine for leprosy.

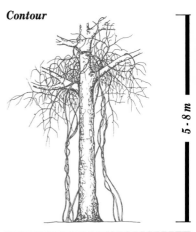

Contour

5 - 8 m

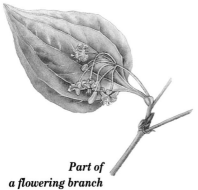

Part of
a flowering branch

Use

Bristly greenbrier is especially suitable for covering old trees but also for different kinds of walls. As its tendrils are tiny, a support must be made of thin elements (wire, metal netting). The fruits provide food for birds.

Bristly greenbrier

Site

Bristly greenbrier is very heat-loving and grows reliably only in the warmest temperature zones, A and B. At exceptionally suitable, sheltered sites it can also be grown in temperature zone C.

Cultivation

Its cultivation does not require any special care. It is not absolutely necessary to water the plant during lengthy dry spells. The seedlings should preferably be planted in autumn and after planting, the branches should be tied to a support. It is advisable to cover young plants with leaves and green brushwood for the winter.

Thin, sharp thorns do not develop on new branches until later, when the fruit is ripening.

Riverbank Grape

Vitis riparia

This plant is a luxuriant and fast-growing plant that can reach a height of 15 m. Its fruits are purple to black in colour, and although the fruits are edible they have no economic significance as they are extremely tart. The tiny, yellow-green flowers develop at the end of May and flower till the end of June. They have a very intensive reseda scent and are sometimes used for flavouring wine-and-fruit drinks. Riverbank grape also looks splendid in autumn when the colour of its leaves turns a beautiful golden yellow.

Use and site

Riverbank grape is quite suitable for large pergolas and walls, noise barriers, and for columns and poles. It can also creep along old tree trunks. Its fruits are eaten by birds and flower provide food for bees.

This is a modest species. It grows well in permeable, sometimes stony soils. A high calcium content in the soil is desirable (ground calcium or old crushed plaster can be added). The plant also stands drought well and unlike European grape, it is quite hardy. It can also be grown in very cold regions and tolerates the frosts of temperature zone E.

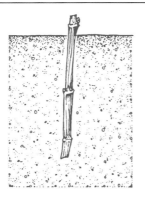

Most Vitis species can be quite easily propagated from hardwood cuttings inserted in the soil.

8 - 15 m

Contour

A flowering branch

Cultivation

The plant tolerates drought well and watering is usually unnecessary. On large surfaces, riverbank grape may be allowed to grow quite freely. If it is exceptionally damaged by frost or if it forms too large a mass, it may be pruned quite substantially without suffering damage, and it will grow well again.

Riverbank grape can be propagated very easily by about 40-cm-long hardwood cuttings which should be cut in autumn or at the beginning of winter. The cuttings should be stored in wet sand in a cool cellar or placed into a groove in a bed outdoors and covered with leaves or compost. In spring cuttings should be inserted into the soil after removing their lower buds.

European Grape

Vitis vinifera

In vineyards, this species is pruned to obtain a low climbing shrub. When allowed to grow freely, it is very vigorous and can quickly reach a height of 20 m. In vineyards, many varieties are cultivated for their delicious fruit, but grown on a wall, it can be beautiful as well as useful. It forms a green cover as splendid as other climbers. In autumn its leaves turn orang-red and there are, of course, its delicious grapes.

Bunch of European grape

Site and cultivation

European grape requires a warm and sunny site. It likes calcium. Its cultivation limit coincides with that of temperature zone C, as shown on the map in the introduction.

European grape tolerates drought well and watering is usually not required. This plant is susceptible to fungal diseases against which chemical sprays must be often used.

A good yield may be obtained by special pruning. In principle,

Use

European grape is the result of selective breeding and cultivation for perhaps several millennia and it is one of the oldest cultivated plants. It is already mentioned in the Jewish Torah, which formed the basis for the Christian Old Testament. Its origin probably lies in the Caucasus. The plant is quite suitable for large pergolas, and southern walls.

Contour

10 - 20 m

Annual shoot of European grape

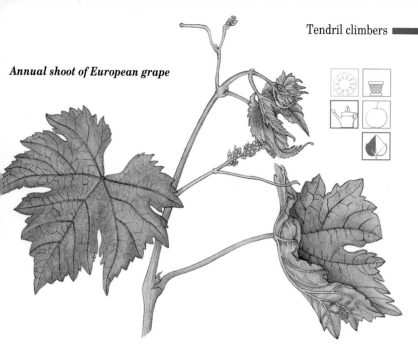

European grape flowers and bears fruit on the branches growing out of the previous year's wood and the previous year's wood grows from that of the year before. The methods of cultivating European grape have been described in specialised literature.

Phylloxera vastatrix is a dangerous pest, which damages rootstocks. Therefore in most of Europe only grapes grafted onto resistant rootstocks can be grown and transport of seedlings is restricted by phyto-quarantine regulations even within countries.

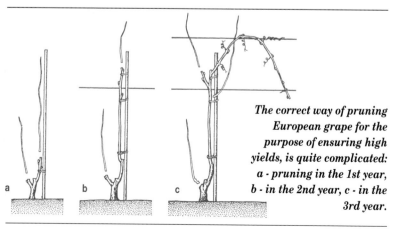

The correct way of pruning European grape for the purpose of ensuring high yields, is quite complicated: a - pruning in the 1st year, b - in the 2nd year, c - in the 3rd year.

Tendril climbers with adhesive pads

Tendril climbers with adhesive pads have the most perfect and the most specialised organs for clinging to their supports. The tendrils form small swellings covered with a sticky substance at their ends. Touching a support they stick to it, turning into flat discs by means of which the plant is fixed extremely firmly even to a completely smooth surface. Each tendril then contracts serpent-like, drawing its branch still more tightly to its support.

Requirements for a support

Because of their tendrils with adhesive pads, these climbers do not require any supports and they have only minimum demands on the surface they are to cover. The surface may be quite smooth, but it must always be firm enough. Crumbly and peeling plaster should either be repaired or removed completely and only bare brickwork should be left. Lime plaster should be perfectly carbonised and should not be wiped off. The adhesive pads usually do not cling to whitewashed walls.

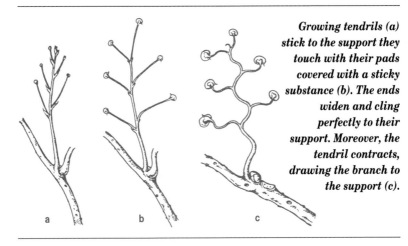

Growing tendrils (a) stick to the support they touch with their pads covered with a sticky substance (b). The ends widen and cling perfectly to their support. Moreover, the tendril contracts, drawing the branch to the support (c).

a   b   c

A brick wall is an ideal base for tendril climbers with adhesive pads.

Use

The species with adhesive pads are particularly suitable for vast areas without windows, for noise barriers, walls, retaining walls etc. On such surfaces their ability to spread laterally and to provide a uniform cover for large surfaces without the need for support may be utilised best of all.

These species are less suitable for walls with windows and for all places where the spreading of a plant cover outside a determined area is undesirable. What you save on supports would have to be spent on regular yearly pruning later on.

These species are unsuitable for whitewashed walls, to which they do not cling.

Virginia Creeper
Parthenocissus quinquefolia

The plant is native to the east of the North American continent, where it grows on forest edges from New York down to Florida. It is not remarkable for either its flowers or its fruits. It is cultivated particularly for its ability to overgrow and cover large surfaces quickly without any need for supports. It is also popular for the beautiful red colour of its leaves in autumn and for its modest demands.

Use

The original species does not produce many adhesive pads, some branches stick out from their support and hang down backwards. Some varieties which have a larger number of tendrils with adhesive pads are also outstanding for their very flat, sessile growth. This goes especially for *P. quinquefolia* var. *murorum* and *P. quinquefolia* var. *saint-paulii*.

Virginia creeper is quite suitable for walls, retaining walls and pergolas. It also looks well on columns and poles. It is able to cover fences quickly, screening them well from view. It is also worth cultivating in pots on terraces and balconies. It is a melliferous plant - bees swarm to it during the flowering period, and in autumn its fruit provides food for birds.

Contour

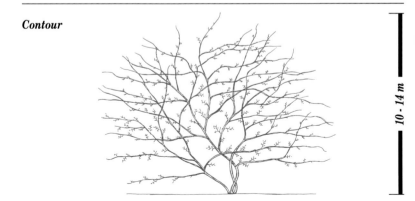

10 - 14 m

A branch with fruits and with leaves turning to autumn colours

Site

This is a modest species. It likes sunshine but does not mind partial shade. However, the more sunshine it receives the more beautiful the colours of its leaves in autumn. It grows well in any kind of common garden soil and also does well in stony soil. It is very hardy and can also be grown in cooler regions - it tolerates the frosts of temperature zone E quite well.

Cultivation

If it spreads too much it can be pruned as required. It also tolerates a pruning of its old wood well and will grow again very rapidly after being pruned substantially. Its seedlings can be planted both in spring and in autumn. Similarly to riverbank grape, Virginia creeper can also be propagated from hardwood cuttings inserted directly into the ground.

Japanese Creeper

Parthenocissus tricuspidata

This species is not remarkable for its flowers or fruits. Its qualities are similar to those of the previous species. It grows very fast. Its tendrils with adhesive pads are usually very well developed and the plant forms even a more sessile and flatter cover than the previous species. The trilobate leaves look like roof tiles in the way they sit on the wall and they cover any wall perfectly. The beautiful red colour of the leaves in autumn is striking. Japanese creeper is native to Japan, central China and Korea.

Use

Japanese creeper also exists in several cultivars. The 'Veitchii' cultivar with an especially sessile and flat growth is the best known. Other cultivars are grown only very rarely. This plant is quite suitable for walls and noise barriers, various columns and poles. It is able to cover fences quickly, screening them perfectly from view. It has also been shown that the plant is worth cultivating in pots on terraces and balconies. Like the previous species, it provides nectar for bees and food for birds.

Contour

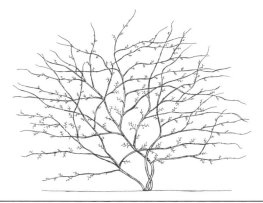

12 - 16 m

Leaf colours in autumn

Site

It likes sunshine but does not mind partial shade. However, the more sunshine the plant receives, the more intensive the red colour of the leaves is in autumn. Japanese creeper also grows in partial shade but then its leaves do not colour at all. It can easily be grown in any kind of common garden soil and will also make do with stony soil. It can be planted both in spring and autumn. Japanese creeper is very hardy, it can also be grown in cooler regions, and tolerates the frosts of temperature zone E well.

Cultivation

The plant does not require any special care. It can be pruned as required. It also tolerates a pruning of its old wood very well and will grow again very rapidly after being pruned substantially. Unlike the previous species the attempts to propagate it by cuttings have failed and you should buy seedlings which can be planted either in spring or in autumn.

Climbing annuals

They are as varied a group of climbers as woody climbers. In botanical terminology "annuals" are plants which grow from seed, flower, bear fruit and die within the same year. However, in gardening practice the term "annuals" covers all plants which are not able to overwinter outside and must be planted anew every year, even if in their native regions they may be continually growing woody plants.

Climbing annuals do not grow as big as woody climbers within a single year, but they have other qualities. They are suitable for covering smaller supports - fences and rails, and for being cultivated in pots on balconies, etc. They flower very soon after planting and provide an almost immediate effect. Soil enrichment need not be as

An example of a portable wooden pot with a supporting screen for cultivating climbing annuals

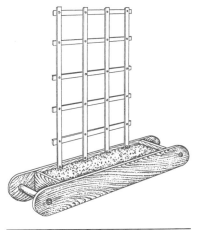

thorough because they grow at the site for one year only. They are cheap and may be used as temporary covers for unsightly corners. At places where they are used for several years different species can be grown each year.

Supports

The supports for annuals should also respect the way in which the plants cling to their supports. Annuals attach practically only by twining or by using their tendrils. The supports for annuals may be quite simple. Twining species will use thin bars or strings and annual tendril climbers can climb directly along wire fences or screens.

Use of annuals

Climbing annuals are especially suitable for being planted into larger boxes or pots, for balconies and for all places where a quick effect is to be attained. The pots may be substantially smaller than those for woody climbers - many species will do with common windowboxes. Robust and moisture-

Although woody climbers can also be grown in pots,
for balconies annuals are more usual.

requiring species (e.g. cup-and-saucer
plant and japanese hop) should
preferably be cultivated in tubs or larger
containers (of at least 30x30x30 cm).

Cup-and-Saucer Plant

Cobaea scandens

The plant was named after Barnabas Cobo, the Spanish priest and scholar (1582-1657). It is one of the most robust climbers that are cultivated in Europe as annuals. Over summer it may easily reach a height of 6 m. In its tropical native region it overwinters (it is native to Mexico and Costa Rica), but in the temperate zone it is not able to overwinter outdoors and should therefore be planted anew as an annual every year.

The pinnate leaves end in tendrils that are able to cling to a rough support by themselves. However, their grip is not firm and it is advisable to prepare a simple support for the plant. A sufficiently firm string will suffice. The flowers are interesting. They flower from August till the first frosts, that is at a time when other plants have nothing but their fruits to adorn them. The colours of the flowers are also remarkable. The flower buds and newly opened, bell-shaped flowers are creamy white. Later the flowers turn dark and before being shed they become violet-purple.

Use and site

This plant is quite suitable for covering fences, pergolas and various types of wall, and for cultivating in pots on balconies and terraces, in temperature zones A to D. It requires full sunshine and good soil enriched with fertilisers.

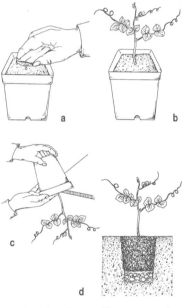

Raising the seedlings: a - sowing the seeds in a pot in February, b - raising at a temperature of around 18 °C, c - taking the seedlings out of the pot, d - planting in soil (in a large pot).

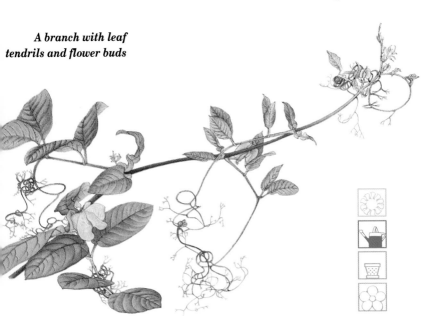

A branch with leaf tendrils and flower buds

Cultivation

You should fertilise these plants occasionally with mixed fertilisers and water them adequately and regularly, especially when they are grown in pots.

The seedlings are raised in greenhouses from the end of February and they can be planted outdoors only when the danger of late spring frosts is over. The seeds can also be sown in a pot at home at the beginning of March.

Flowers and their successive colour changes

Mock Cucumber

Echinocystis lobata

This very vigorously growing "real" annual is related to cucumbers and gourds. Its herbaceous stems quickly reach a length of 5 m. It has fresh green palmatilobate leaves with a shape remindful of maple leaves. The cream male flowers are arranged in rich clusters. The female flowers, which turn later into the fruits, grow on the same plant as the male ones, but singly, in the leaf axils. The ovoid fruits are yellow-green berries covered with soft spines. They are about 3-5 cm in diameter and usually contain 4 seeds. The plant clings firmly to fences, screens and other supports by means of its tendrils. It is native to the North American continent.

Use and site

Mock cucumber is quite suitable for covering fences, screening them perfectly from view, for pergolas and various types of wall and also for growing in pots on balconies and terraces in temperature zones A to D. It requires a site in full sunshine or partial shade.

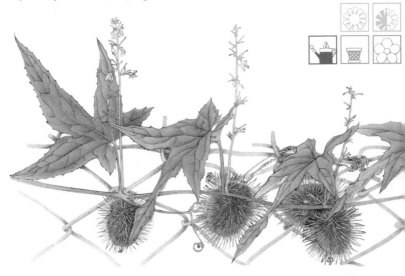

Cultivation

This plant requires adequate and regular watering, particularly when it is grown in pots. It is also advisable to fertilise the plants with mixed fertilisers occasionally. At the end of March two to three seeds should be sown in each pot filled with good garden soil and they should be watered well. They germinate very quickly at a temperature of around 20 °C and when the danger of late spring frosts is over they can be planted outdoors. They can also be sown outdoors at the beginning of May. In that case, of course, the plants flower somewhat later. This plant tends to be overlooked by garden shops and so the seeds are hard to come by. In spite of that, in some regions mock cucumber is grown a lot. In those districts it should not be hard to get some seed.

*A male flower cluster,
fruit and seeds*

*A branch with male flowers
and with fruits at different
stages of development*

Japanese Hop

Humulus japonicus

This is also a vigorously growing annual. It grows very fast and creates green walls up to 6 m high. The male flowers are inconspicuous; the female ones are arranged in tiny green cones. The hairy, rough leaves remain deep green till late in autumn. They do not produce tendrils but twine around a suitable support. Apart from the basic species with green leaves, a variety with white variegated leaves is also often grown. As its name suggests, Japanese hop is native to Japan.

Use

The plant is quite suitable for pergolas, and for various walls fitted with simple supports. It also looks well on columns, rails and high fences. It can also be easily grown in pots on balconies and terraces.

Site

It likes both sunshine and partial shade in temperature zones A to D. It grows well in any kind of garden soil and will do with poor-quality soil if the soil is moist enough. The variegated variety requires more light and should be grown only in full sunshine.

Cultivation

The plant requires adequate and regular watering, especially when it is grown in pots. It is also advisable to fertilise potted plants with mixed fertilisers occasionally. In March two to three seeds should be sown in each pot with good garden soil and they should be watered well. They germinate at a temperature of 18-20 °C. The small seedlings should be trained along thin sticks stuck into pots right at the start. They should be planted outdoors only when the danger of late spring frosts is over. They can be sown outdoors in

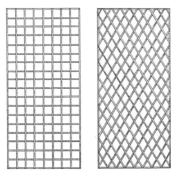

Examples of suitable supports

their final growing position at the end of April. In that case, of course, the plants will grow somewhat later.

Japanese hop

Tricolor Morning Glory

Ipomoea tricolor

This very popular climbing annual is native to Mexico. It twists around a support (string, wire) up to a height of 3-5 metres but it does not spread laterally very much and thus does not look robust. From June till autumn it produces large numbers of wide trumpet-shaped flowers. Each flower lasts for one day only, and changes colour during the day, which is typical of this species. In the morning when the flowers develop they are red, then they change their colour, and in the evening before being shed they are light blue. The fading flowers are replaced by new ones the next day. Apart from this basic species garden cultivars exist with differently coloured flowers.

Use and site

Tricolor morning glory is quite suitable for walls fitted with simple supports made for instance of tight strings. It is impressive especially near entrances or when it is used for dividing large areas. It looks fine on columns as well. It can also be easily grown in pots on balconies and terraces.

The plant should be protected from draughts and situated in full sunshine. The plant does not tolerate shade. Good garden soil is most suitable but it should not be overfertilised with nitrogen. With excessive nitrogen in the soil, the plant grows vigorously but does not produce many flowers. It is suitable for temperature zones A to D.

Tricolor morning glory trained along a vertically anchored string

*A flowering tricolor morning glory
with flower buds and spent flowers*

Cultivation

Tricolor morning glory requires adequate and regular watering, in particular when it is grown in pots. However, it does not like excessive moisture. The formation of flowers is helped by enriching the soil with potash and phosphorus fertilisers. In March, two to three seeds should be sown in pots with good garden soil and they should be watered well. They germinate at a temperature of 18-20 °C. The seedlings should be trained along thin sticks stuck into the pots right at the start. The seedlings should be planted outdoors only when the danger of late spring frosts is over. The seeds can be sown in their final growing position in the middle of May.

Sweet Pea

Lathyrus odoratus

Sweet pea has been cultivated since the beginning of the 18th century. It is not as robust as the preceding annuals. Its height depends on the variety and usually ranges between 130 and 200 cm.

Sweet pea is cultivated particularly for its numerous pleasantly scented flowers. The original species had only 2-3 flowers on each peduncle. Today's cultivars have 6-8 of them on each peduncle. The peduncle is long and the flowers can be cut to be put in a vase, where they may last for as long as a week. The colour range of the flowers is very broad and perhaps only yellow is not included. The plant climbs by means of its leaf tendrils.

Use and site

Sweet pea is especially suitable for covering fences. It grows well in pots on balconies and terraces. Wire netting is the most suitable support.

Sweet pea requires a sunny situation protected from draughts. Good garden soil with a sufficient calcium content is best, and temperature zones A to E are suitable.

Cultivation

The plant is sensitive to drought and requires adequate and regular watering, especially when it is grown in pots, in which the soil dries out quickly.

The seeds should be sown directly in the ground - into a shallow groove along a fence or another support at a distance of about 10 cm. Sowing should usually start at the end of March and in warmer regions even earlier. Sweet pea sown in April starts flowering by the middle of June. It flowers for about two months, and sowing at intervals will ensure the plant flowers till autumn. Cut flowers in a vase last long. Cutting them also promotes the development of new flowers. Morning is the best time for cutting them.

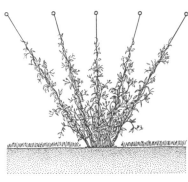

Sweet pea can be trained along strings into a fan shape.

Sweet pea in flower

Butterfly Runner

Phaseolus coccineus

This well-known and vigorously growing plant is native to South America. It grows very rapidly, forming green walls up to 4 m high. The flowers are arranged in multiple-flower racemes on long petioles. Apart from the plants with scarlet flowers species with red and white or purely white flowers also exist. The plant comes into flower from July till September. It does not form tendrils but twines around a suitable support.

Red and white flowers

Use

The plant is quite suitable for pergolas, various types of wall fitted with simple supports. It also looks well on columns, rails and high fences. It can easily be grown in pots on balconies and terraces.

All raw beans contain toxic proteins. These substances are rendered harmless by boiling and therefore beans have to be cooked to make them edible. The pods and black dotted seeds of ornamental butterfly runner are also edible after they are boiled.

Site and cultivation

Butterfly runner requires sunshine. It grows well in any kind of garden soil and does not mind poor-quality soil. It needs sufficient moisture to grow quickly. It is suitable for being cultivated in temperature zones A to E.

The plant does not require any special care, apart from regular

Typical cluster of red flowers

watering, especially when it is grown in pots. It is also advisable to enrich the pot soil with mixed fertilisers now and then. Four to six seeds should be sown in little hollows made in the ground. The seeds can be sown when the danger of late spring frosts is over. The young plants can also be raised in pots.

A pod with ripe seeds

Black-eyed Clockvine

Thunbergia alata

This is a perennial in the tropical zone to which it is native (it comes from the coast of southern Africa), but in Europe it can overwinter only in a greenhouse or in a room, and outdoors it is cultivated only as an annual. The yellow flowers with their velvet black centres ("eyes") are the plant's greatest attraction.

The word "eye" also appears in the popular names of the new cultivars which have different colours (white, cream or orange) and sometimes lack the black centres. This charming plant was named after Pehr K. Thunberg, the Swedish collector and natural scientist (1743-1822). He travelled throughout the South African continent, Java and Japan and became a professor of natural sciences in Uppsala.

Use and Site

Black-eyed clockvine does not form any tendrils - it twines around its support (a string or pole) up to a height of 2 m. It can also be grown as an indoor plant. Outdoors, it is suitable for being grown in pots on balconies, verandas and terraces. It also looks splendid on sunny walls and around entrances. It requires a site situated in full sunshine and with good soil enriched with fertilisers and containing calcium. It is suitable for temperature zones A to D.

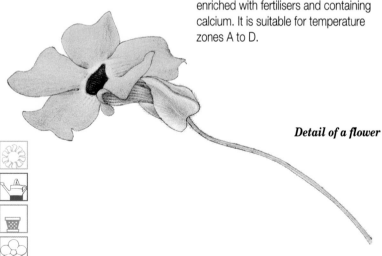

Detail of a flower

Cultivation

This plant should occasionally be treated with mixed fertilisers and should be watered adequately and regularly, especially when it is grown in pots. You should raise the seedlings in a greenhouse beginning from March. The seedlings can be transplanted outdoors only when the danger of late spring frosts is over. At the beginning of March the seeds can also be sown in a pot indoors and raised in a light place near a window at a temperature of 18-20 °C. The seedlings should be trained along thin poles inserted into the pots right from the start.

A box with a bar support. When it is overgrown with plants it forms a beautiful flower column.

Black-eyed clockvine climbing upwards along poles

Common Nasturtium

Tropaeolum majus

This plant is native to Chile, Peru and Colombia, where it is often a perennial. It has been cultivated as a great number of cultivars, some of which only grow as upright shrubs. The orange, yellow or vermilion and scarlet flowers develop from June till the first frosts. The round leaves with petioles in their centres also have an interesting structure. Common nasturtium does not twine around its support and it does not form tendrils but utilises its leaf petioles, and that very imperfectly. Therefore it is not able to twist along a string or wire but needs netting or a screen.

The flowers of two colored varieties

Use

The plant is suitable for being grown in pots on balconies and terraces and in window boxes. It can also be planted above various types of retaining walls and small terraces from which it hangs down. It can climb along wire fences. Common nasturtium is also used for cooking. Its young leaves have a hot radish taste, they contain plenty of vitamins and are edible. Its flowers can be used for decorating food, the flower buds can be pickled as capers. The plant also has pharmaceutical applications.

Cultivation and site

Common nasturtium requires full sunshine but also tolerates partial shade. It requires adequate and regular watering, especially when it is grown in pots. Occasionally treating the soil with

Common nasturtium

phosphorus fertilisers will help it flower. Nitrogenous fertilisers should be avoided because they give lush growth but little flower. In the middle of May and in warmer regions even earlier, 2-3 seeds should be sown in the final growing position spaced 40-50 cm apart. Approximately a month before planting, the seedlings may also be raised in a greenhouse or at home near a window at a temperature of 18-20 °C. They should be planted outdoors only when the danger of late spring frosts is over. The plants are often attacked by aphids, against which special sprays should be used.

The seeds are an important component of some medicinal teas.

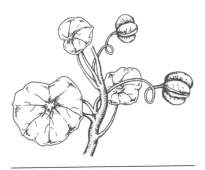

Canary Creeper

Tropaeolum peregrinum

Canary creeper is also a most attractive species. It has glossy, yellow flowers with fringed upper petals which develop in large numbers from June till autumn. This species does not twine around its support or form any specialised tendrils but it makes perfect use of its leaf petioles. Along netting it climbs up to a height of 4 m. It is native to Peru and Ecuador, from where it was brought to the Canary Islands around the year 1720 and escaped into the wild.

Use

The plant is quite suitable for smaller pergolas and various types of wall. It overgrows fences, screening them from view in a most attractive way. It also grows well in pots on balconies and terraces. It is not for use as an overhanging plant.

Site

Unlike other nasturtiums, this species prefers partial shade to sunshine. It grows in any kind of garden soil if it has sufficient moisture. Both nasturtium species are suitable for being cultivated in temperature zones A to D.

A detail of interesting fringed flowers

A leaf detail

A flowering branch

Cultivation

The plant does not require any special care apart from adequate and regular watering, especially when it is grown in pots. The treatment of the plant with phosphorus fertilisers occasionally helps it flower. Nitrogenous fertilisers give lush growth but not much flower. The seeds germinate slowly and therefore it is advisable to use raised seedlings for outdoor planting. They can be grown from seeds sown in a greenhouse or at home near a window at a temperature of 18-20 °C about a month before planting. They can be planted outdoors only when the danger of late spring frosts is over. At the beginning of May, 2-3 seeds can also be sown at distances of 40-50 cm in the final growing position. Plants grown from seeds sown outdoors flower later.

Index